The Happy Satanist
Finding Self-Empowerment

Lilith Starr

To Zac —
So glad you are
in this world with
me!

☿ Love, ♡

Lilith Starr ✦

THE HAPPY SATANIST

Finding Self-Empowerment

Lilith Starr

LILITH STARR STUDIOS
Publishing Division
3400 Harbor Avenue Southwest, Suite 109
Seattle, Washington 98126

ORDERING INFORMATION
Quantity Sales
*Special discounts are available on quantity purchases
by corporations, associations, and others.
For details, contact the publisher at the address above.*

Orders by U.S. Trade Bookstores and Wholesalers
Please contact the publisher at the address above.

First Printing, 2015
Lilith Starr Studios

ISBN: 1501021737
ISBN-13: 978-1501021732

DEDICATION

*To Uruk Black, devoted slaveboi,
husband, and priest.*

*Thank you for bringing me back
to life with your love.*

FOREWORD

by Melanie Strong

I first met Lilith about 15 years ago at one of her infamous S&M parties. I wasn't into S&M myself but I found her a warm and welcoming host who made sure everyone was happy and comfortable. I was pleased that we became friends. We lost touch when I moved out of the country but have recently found each other again online and I am happy to be able to reconnect.

It was difficult to hear about the hard time she'd been through, but I was amazed at her courage and resilience to keep fighting no matter what. I think many people would have given up long ago in similar circumstances.

I first read these essays when they were published online. I don't consider myself to be a Satanist, but I do understand their philosophy. I think these essays offer a very personal and moving account of the positive effects that their philosophy can have on individuals and society. Contained in these essays are stories of battles, the lowest of the lows and also great hope.

Lilith went through dark times but was able to empower herself with the skills and wisdom to make it through those times and build a new life for her and her love. Now she is sharing her experiences and what she has learned with others in the hopes of being able to encourage and help them.

I believe that there is much people can learn from these essays; courage, hope, wisdom, and love shine through them. I believe they will offer readers an insightful glimpse into a belief system that is often misunderstood at best and vilified at worst. Often when we read about another's journey we find guidance for our own. While our circumstances are different, there is a truth that can speak to us and help us in our own path. This has been my experience reading these essays and I hope it is yours too.

CONTENTS

INTRODUCTION

I wrote these essays over 2012 to 2013 for the Facebook Satanism page, where I was the editor-in-chief. It was an exciting time. Social media had suddenly exploded, and Satanists from all walks of life and all corners of the globe were finally coming together on a public forum. We grabbed the chance to educate many of the curious and provide a public face for the modern Satanism movement.

In these fellow Satanists I found the most honest, kind, clear-headed people I've ever met. Daring to write about Satanism openly on a public forum took a certain amount of guts. It was rewarding to see actual Satanic issues openly discussed, instead of suppressed by a fearful media and a judgemental theocracy.

Now in 2015, Satanism has really come into the limelight as a formidable weapon to fight for the separation of church and state. The Satanic Temple is currently making headline after headline as they show up the hypocrisy of Christian legislation, demanding equal rights for Satanists wherever Christianity is inserted into our governments, schools and laws. I joined the Temple and was recently chosen to head its Seattle chapter.

I'm proud to be part of a movement that dares to stand up to the increasingly shrill voices of the American theocracy, the intolerant religious bigots, and the abusers who use Christianity as an excuse for their evils.

Satanism has also played a central, very personal role in my own life, allowing me to finally blossom into my full potential. The self-empowerment at the core of the philosophy gave me the inner strength I needed to beat a lifetime of addiction, including a near-fatal heroin addiction. It gave me the impetus to seek effective treatment for my severe clinical depression and finally find the right combination of psych meds, meditation and exercise to heal my broken mind and body.

And it's given me the strength to keep going even in the face of debilitating chronic pain. Every day, my pain threatens to take me down, but my passion and personal drive keep me living the meaningful life I've always dreamed of. I have at my command all the power that lies within me, without needing to depend on outside sources or authorities.

Satanism was exactly what I needed to shake the self-hatred that had derailed me at every step since childhood. These essays are my gift of gratitude to the philosophy that finally brought the healing and recovery I'd desperately sought for 39 years. I hope you enjoy reading them as much as I enjoyed writing them.

MY SATANIC BELIEFS

I believe that I am the highest power in my own life, which entails not only self-empowerment, but self-responsibility.

I believe that I and all beings deserve compassion, self-compassion and freedom from shame and stigma.

I believe in the Seven Fundamental Tenets of the Satanic Temple:

- *One should strive to act with compassion and empathy towards all creatures in accordance with reason.*
- *The struggle for justice is an ongoing and necessary pursuit that should prevail over laws and institutions.*
- *One's body is inviolable, subject to one's own will alone.*
- *The freedoms of others should be respected, including the freedom to offend. To willfully and unjustly encroach upon the freedoms of another is to forgo your own.*
- *Beliefs should conform to our best scientific understanding of the world. We should take care never to distort scientific facts to fit our beliefs.*
- *People are fallible. If we make a mistake, we should do our best to rectify it and resolve any harm that may have been caused.*
- *Every tenet is a guiding principle designed to inspire nobility in action and thought. The spirit of compassion, wisdom, and justice should always prevail over the written or spoken word.* [1]

I believe in the self-organizing and emergent nature of complex systems at all levels of the universe, including inside us. I believe reality is miraculous and sacred all on its own, with no God required to create it.

As Peter Gilmore of the Church of Satan says,

"Satanists do not believe in the supernatural, in neither God nor the Devil. To the Satanist, he is his own God. … The reality behind Satan is simply the dark evolutionary force of entropy that permeates all of nature and provides the drive for survival and propagation inherent in all living things. Satan is not a conscious entity to be worshiped, rather a reservoir of power inside each human to be tapped at will." [2]

WHY I AM A SATANIST

I AM A SATANIST . . .

- Because I cannot stand by idly while children are raped and abused, women subjugated and beaten and human beings seeded with self-hate and shame in the name of religion. I must call out what I see.

- Because our very world, the environment that sustains us, is being destroyed and our future along with it, and those who stand in the way of addressing this are doing it in the name of God and the almighty dollar.

- Because every day in my country, laws are created that give privilege to religious beliefs of corporations over the rights of individuals.

- Because I've known too many friends who suffered horribly at the hands of abusive parents who used religion as a weapon, destroying their children's sanity and capacity for self-compassion, leaving only shame, hurt, and self-hate.

- Because I believe in individual liberty, the foundation of my country centuries ago. I believe in seeing it restored, taken back from the hands of the corporations and the theocracy.

- Because I believe in science, and I believe science and cooperation are our greatest hope to save our race and / or avoid untold suffering in the coming climate disaster. I believe science trumps blind faith in every way, and its value should not be up for debate.

- Because I believe that every human being on this planet deserves love, compassion and connection, regardless of their race, religion, class, sexual orientation, gender, or any other meaningless category beyond "human being."

- Because I believe compassion and working together will get us much farther than judgement, shame and fear. I believe that we are wired naturally for cooperation and compassion, along with our other healthy animal instincts, and when we shed the chains of religious slavery and accept our true natures, we will become whole again.

- Because I believe we are not intrinsically bad, destined to burn in hell for trivial offenses to a non-existent god. I believe we deserve self-compassion and self-forgiveness, along with accepting self-responsibility and recognizing our own power over our lives.

- Because like the mythological Satan and Lilith, I have chosen to use my voice to speak up in the face of arbitrary authority, and I refuse to be silenced, subjugated or bowed.

FINDING SATANISM

I have always taken the road less travelled. Eventually that road led me to Satanism, where I found the wisdom and the power to integrate and heal myself.

I was conceived one night in a farm field under the stars, most likely while my parents were on acid. They were counter-culture rebels and back-to-the-land hippies. They rejected the city and the rest of society and struck out on their own to build a different kind of life.

Until I was 12, we lived isolated from civilization on 40 acres of lonely wilderness in far Northern California. We grew all our own food and lived without electricity, phone service, or plumbing. I had no siblings and no friends — just the forest to keep me company.

From the very beginning, I didn't fit in with the rest of society. The kids at school told me I was "too smart and too weird." I was the pariah, the outcast in every school I attended until college. So I turned to books, especially science books, for solace. My family was extremely open-minded and not Christian. I was allowed to ask questions and feed my hungry, curious mind. I started writing in second grade and went on to win a number of writing awards in my school years.

I continued my love affair with science through high school, and upon graduation I was granted a full scholarship to Harvard University to become a genetic engineer. After my first year there, I realized I wanted to become a writer instead, returning to my beloved wordsmithing. I switched to English, earned my bachelor's degree and went on to earn my master's degree in journalism at Stanford.

Coming out of Stanford, I immediately got hired into the tech industry as a journalist. Life was one success after another, at least in the work world. I saw the web coming early on and my many stints at short-lived web startups paid off with a high-level editorial position at Amazon.com. I had an office with a view, a crack team of writers that I managed, a giant house on a hill and more stock money than I knew what to do with.

But my beautiful life held a dark secret: my untreated depression still dogged me. I had become deeply addicted to huffing nitrous oxide gas while at Stanford. The depression drove me back to addiction again and again, draining my savings and shattering my self-esteem. When the dot-com bubble burst around 2001, I started going rapidly downhill. I had quit the office to become a high-paid consultant, but my work began to dry up, helped by my increasingly severe depression and out-of-control drug use.

By 2007 I had quit or lost all my corporate jobs and was barely surviving on doing wedding photography, domination, and erotic massage. I reached a point where I gave up. I had tried for 15 years to shake the nitrous addiction, but nothing worked. I figured I was a waste of a human being and it would be best for me to sink down into the addiction and depression until I flickered out in a slow suicide.

But fate had other plans. I met the most honest, kind man on the planet, my husband Uruk. He was a lifelong Satanist. We had an informal relationship at first, trying to juggle polyamory with our existing partners. We got to see each other once a week. But that was enough to spark huge changes in me.

Uruk did not judge or belittle me; he accepted me exactly as I was. His simple, uncomplicated, undemanding acceptance changed my world. Shortly after we got together, I set down the nitrous addiction for good. I had found something much better: him! And in his eyes, I had found myself as I truly was, not the failure or addict everyone else had labelled me as. That was enough to break the chains I had thought would be with me to the end.

Throwing everything I had to the wind, I skipped our small rural town with him and we went to the San Francisco Bay Area in search of a new life, leaving all our possessions and friends behind.

It was not a friendly place to start over. The housing market in San Francisco was the most insane in the US, with a one-bedroom apartment costing over $3,000/month. My plan was to work doing erotic massage in hotels until we could save up money for housing, but the hotels we could afford didn't allow any visitors. So we tried renting rooms in people's houses, but that turned out to be a nightmare in and of itself, partly because I couldn't work there.

After two dishonest landlords dumped us out overnight, we ended up homeless on the streets.

I thought the slow death of my addiction in my comfortable apartment had been bad. I had no idea what bad was until we were actually homeless.

Living on the streets, you have zero options to pull yourself up. There is nowhere to charge your cell phone. Food? Meds that you need to not go insane? Simply the right to exist? It seems you deserve none of this once you are homeless.

The very worst part wasn't the practical considerations, but rather the way society treated us. As a homeless person, everyone who passes by makes it very clear that you are lower than the cockroach or the rat, the lowest kind of vermin. You get treated like a piece of shit, not a human being. Basic survival is denied you, let alone compassion, help and human dignity.

I saw the true face of society, and it was very ugly. We were an inconvenience getting in the way of everyone's rush to the Starbucks drivethrough, a pest control problem, a piece of trash that needed to be taken away. We were treated worse than criminals or baby-rapers. It was as if our existence was a personal affront to every normal person, a cancer that had to be wiped out.

Besides this, I was literally insane. I was unable to get my antidepressant, Paxil. Paxil has some of the worst withdrawal symptoms, like insanity and suicide. I was on the streets, crazy, driven from place to place by the cops. One morning I threw myself down at the feet of a cop, sobbing, begging her to just shoot me. After just three days, I was ready to end it all. My husband and I agreed to find some heroin and kill ourselves.

But before we could do that, an old friend from high school managed to contact me on the last of our phone battery. He saved our lives: he paid for a cheap motel for a couple of months. I was shell-shocked, insane, unable to do anything but lay in the hotel room and cling to Uruk in horror, too crazy to start rebuilding my life from scratch.

THE SATANIC CONVERSION

It was at this point that I picked up my husband's Satanic Bible and read it cover to cover, following it with the Satanic Rituals (both by Anton LaVey). I had nothing else to do but be crazy. I was trying to find work and stability, but I was far too insane, paralyzed in a cheap motel bed that might as well have been my deathbed.

In these books, I found the first glimmers of hope. The ideas there planted the seeds that would eventually blossom into full recovery. I realized that I couldn't count on society, on other people, on the system, to take care of me. I saw our society was a spectacular failure on a public level. We were on a tour of the apocalypse, and the hell was even more horrific than I could imagine. I had thought people basically just and kind, and my enlightenment to the evil of mankind was enough to unseat my mind all by itself.

I opened my mind to the concepts laid out by LaVey. I felt the veils of society and tradition lifting from my eyes. I realized that society had never accepted me, so why should I try any longer to fit myself into its mold?

The hardest part of my "conversion" was coming face to face with my self-hate and overcoming my belief that I was a worthless, addicted, homeless failure, someone who needed to sacrifice her happiness for others. While I intellectually grasped the concept of autotheism at the time, that I was indeed the God of my own world, the self-hate that had been so deeply planted in me over the years had deep roots. It would take some time for the seeds of

Satanic empowerment to grow and choke out those outdated beliefs.

But the sea change had occurred. As a Satanist, I was no longer blind to the way the human world really was. I could see clearly the hate, evil, injustice and greed that runs the system and crushes the human spirit. I no longer felt beholden to that system, no longer felt like I was part of it or that I could make it better. I had stepped outside of society for good.

In time, friends helped us get a train ticket to Seattle and find housing here. I was able to start working again doing the erotic massage and domination that I enjoyed so much. And I began rebuilding my life in earnest, using my inner Satanic strength to break barrier after barrier. Now three years later, I live a comfortable, stable, happy life with my beloved husband and my best friend, who came to live with us. I have the time and well-being I need to work on my writing and fulfill my duties as the head of the Satanic Temple's Seattle chapter..

I feel immense gratitude for that crazy month in the dirty cramped hotel room, because I would have gone through life with blinders on without it. I found Satanism at exactly the right time, when I was at the end of my rope. I am happy that I've had the chance to write about my personal experiences and to help others explore this highly empowering philosophy.

MYTHBUSTING SATANISM

Satanism is one of the most misunderstood spiritual paths in the world. Myths about us Satanists abound. I want to address a few of the most common.

1: SATANISTS WORSHIP SATAN.

Why would we trade in one set of chains for another? Traditional LaVeyan Satanism posits no divine force other than one's own will, no god but the Self. Certainly we admire Satan as a symbol of the questioning mind, the refusal to serve, the refusal to blindly obey authority. But the empowering core of Satanism is the belief that you, and you alone, are the most powerful force in your particular world.

In proclaiming ourselves to be each our own god, we realize that only we can change our world, make ourselves happy, win material success, or anything else we desire. We break our dependency on an outside power — especially a made-up one like God. We also break free of the fear of an angry, punishing God who deals out eternal torture for the sin of simply being our natural, animal selves.

2: SATANISTS SELL THEIR SOUL IN EXCHANGE FOR MONEY, POWER, OR SEX.

As per Myth #1 above, Satanists don't have anyone they can sell their soul to, except for themselves! The very concept of the immortal soul is anathema to many Satanists, who view it as a made-up tale told by priests to keep people from rising up against their suffering and injustice in this life for fear of missing out on heaven in the next one.

You'd be surprised, however, at the number of

people who visited the Satanism Facebook page looking for the means to sell their soul to Satan. Many were living in desperately poor areas passed by by the flashy progress, consumption and excess of the Western World, and they yearned for the riches they saw squandered elsewhere. Legend tells that Satan can grant riches, sex, power, rock-and-roll talent and more. I understand where these people are coming from. But Satanism holds no magic path to riches.

However, if you sign yourself over to Satanism by realizing completely, fully, without doubt that you are in charge of your life, you will be empowered to make the required changes, do the hard work, and grab life by the balls. When you reclaim your own power, the magic you seek will happen, although perhaps not as fast or not in the same way you imagined it might. All that is necessary is for you to trust yourself.

3: SATANISTS KILL BABIES AND MAKE OTHER HUMAN SACRIFICES.

Alas, this myth refuses to die the final death it so richly deserves. Satanism is still synonymous with baby sacrifice in many ignorant minds, thanks to a baseless rumor that fed people's irrational fears until it blossomed into a full-blown panic in the 1990s.

"Satanic ritual abuse (SRA) was a moral panic that originated in the United States in the 1980s, spreading throughout the country and eventually to many parts of the world, before subsiding in the late 1990s. ... Official investigations produced no evidence of widespread

conspiracies or of the slaughter of thousands. ...
In the latter half of the 1990s interest in SRA
declined and skepticism became the default
position, with only a minority of believers giving
any credence to the existence of SRA." [3]

This unfortunate panic, akin to the Red Scare of
the McCarthy era, has made it even harder for the
Satanist to find understanding and acceptance.

The notion of sacrifice has no place in a worldview where you are god. There is no angry Father-
God to appease with the slaughter of animals. From
a magical perspective, sacrifice is also unnecessary.
You have all the powers you need without killing
another living being.

4: SATANISTS HAVE EVIL SUPER-POWERS.

In fact, we did not sell our soul and receive
supernatural evil powers from Satan. But we do
have powers that many others do not: the powers of
self-empowerment.

Many Satanists are highly effective people in
all spheres of their life, simply because they trust
themselves, their will, their choices and their
abilities. Unfortunately, a common assumption
when any known Satanist achieves success is that
he or she won it using dark infernal powers. But
when you are hobbled by self-doubt and crippled
by Church-dictated ignorance, a self-realized and
confident Satanist can indeed seem possessed of
superhuman powers.

They are the same powers that are our birthright;
as Satanists we simply refuse to give them up to
others: the power to get things done, make choices

aligned with our goals, spot opportunities, and also accept the consequences of our actions. Together, this can be an extremely effective toolset, though not perhaps in the realm of the supernatural.

5: SATANISTS ACT UNETHICALLY.

Ethics come from inside a person, where morals are imposed from an external source (such as the Church). Just because a Satanist rejects the Christian moral code, it doesn't follow that he also has no ethics.

For instance, I reject the moral codes that tell me sex is wrong, shameful and dangerous. I reject the moral codes that tell me as a woman I must be subservient to all men, and the codes telling me there is something inherently wrong and sinful about me simply because I am female. I break the moral codes about profanity and blasphemy all the fucking time, as well as the ones telling me that medicines like cannabis and psilocybin are wrong.

But I have the same ethical core as any human being. I am not driven to steal, kill, or even use hurtful words. I try to help those in need, even when I have little. I follow a practice of deep compassion towards all beings. My Satanic husband has an even bigger heart. I've seen him give away his last few dollars to buy a hungry homeless guy food.

In fact, you might be surprised to find that many Satanists are the kindest, most loving people you know. When you aren't twisted up inside by the self-hate of the fear-based religions, you have a lot more love to give. When you've rejected the hate and lies, your natural self will blossom, and one of the fruits will be an increased capability for love and compassion.

Christians do good out of fear of punishment. Satanists do good because they are good people.

6: SATANISTS ARE RACIST.

I've encountered a small number of Satanists who are also white supremacists. Some extremists see Satanism as an excuse to promote facism and the concept of a master race.

These bigots are taking the patently non-Satanic belief that "we are God, and you are not." This flies directly in the face of Satanic principles. By accepting that you are your own God, you must also accept that others are their own Gods, and not subject to your command or authority.

Groupthink is exactly what Satanism strives to free us from. No sane Satanist would write off an entire chunk of the human population based solely on their skin color or ethnic background. Racism is not an effective tool for success. The concept of a master race is just as anti-Satanic as the concept of a master God. We do not serve outdated hierarchical models like these.

7: SATANISTS TRY TO CONVERT AS MANY PEOPLE AS POSSIBLE SO THEY CAN BRING MORE SOULS TO THEIR DARK LORD.

In fact, most Satanists are extremely reluctant to talk about their path at all. The reasons are obvious: hate, discrimination, misunderstanding, persecution, and worse from the vast majority of the population.

And recruitment is pretty much non-existent, because we don't even believe in a Dark Lord, let alone one that requires a constant diet of fresh souls. Most Satanists I know would just as soon shut the ignorant masses out of their tradition if they could. Satanism carries with it a strong disincentive for conversion in the first place, and its followers don't necessarily want a whole bunch of new, clueless people joining just because they want to shock their Christian family.

You won't see us going door to door in your neighborhood anytime soon, asking "Have you got a minute to hear the word of Satan today?"

8: SATANISM IS INCOMPATIBLE WITH ANY OTHER SPIRITUAL PATH.

Satanism is much more like a philosophy than a religion, and as such it is highly compatible with almost any other spiritual approach except those that demand fearful obedience to a made-up deity. Obviously, Christianity, Judaism and Islam are right out.

But many other paths, including many Eastern practices, do not conflict with Satanic beliefs in the slightest. In fact, there is a strong correlation between Buddhism and Satanism, as I've found in my own personal experience.

I practiced Zen Buddhism for many years, sitting for meditation with a local group of monks every week. My Satanic conversion did nothing to change my Buddhist beliefs; if anything, it strengthened my appreciation for things-as-they-are, reality as opposed to a separate supernatural realm of any kind. In Buddhism, I was also used to thinking of myself as the most powerful agent of change in my life, and recognizing that my actions had consequences: both Satanic beliefs as well.

At my core, I feel the greatest power in the human world is the power of compassion. Compassion has literally saved my life many times. This seems like an inherently Buddhist view at first glance, but it compliments my Satanic views too. I am empowered, and thus it is easy for me to choose compassion instead of fear in my interactions.

I consider myself an atheist and a humanist as well. Sometimes I will answer someone's questions about Satanism by saying something like "It's a fancy form of atheism."

I see the sacredness of things-as-they-are most clearly in the amazing, evolving views of our universe afforded by science. Satanism too teaches us to enjoy the world around us, for it is all we have.

So deciding to be a Satanist doesn't require you to abandon the rest of your spiritual path, unless that path declares rather emphatically that you are not God and that something else is, something you must obey blindly without question. Any other path, especially one that emphasizes inner solutions, curiosity, and thinking for yourself, is completely compatible.

24

TEN SATANIC ACTIVITIES

How can you best explore Satanism for yourself? Try these everyday activities. You might be surprised to find you've already been doing some of them!

1. READ A BOOK.

We all know that the Devil slips in via book learning, right? Readers start getting, well, these ideas. Oppressive religions have focused so much might on banning certain works of the written word because they recognize the danger to themselves. Once someone reads a mind-opening book, one that offers a different perspective or calls into question the long-held assumptions of a society, their mind will continue to think and ponder. They might even arrive at the truth.

Speculative fiction (sci-fi) and other imaginative works are especially transgressive. Robert Heinlein's books take many pokes at the narrow Christian mindset. Harry Potter books are considered Satanic by many ultra-Christians. Many other books are considered obscene or immoral and are still in this day and age banned from school libraries by close-minded communities.

Books like Catcher in the Rye, works from Kurt Vonnegut, Henry Miller, Ernest Hemingway; so many have been censored and banned. Find out what all the fuss is about! Crack open a book and expand your mind.

2. LEARN SOMETHING NEW.

Find out the truth for yourself. Listen to someone with a different perspective than your own. Learn more about what's going on in science. Recent physics breakthroughs will blow your mind. So will self-evolving systems theory.

For centuries, the Church kept a tight handle on learning, just as they did on the written word. Blind faith requires a commitment to ignorance. Now we're out of the dark ages, and the Church can no longer enforce ignorance by removing all access to information. The cracks are beginning to show. The more we reject the path of ignorance and celebrate the path of open knowledge and learning, the more empowered we will be as individuals.

3. DO SOMETHING FORBIDDEN.

The fact that a rule or law exists doesn't mean you should follow it. Many rules exist to keep the rule-makers in power and control.

Try going for a moonlight walk in a beautiful park (illegal in many places). Or use a chemical or plant not manufactured and controlled by big pharma to ease your pain, expand your mind, or just have a good time. Have sex out of wedlock. Use a curse word. As long as you aren't hurting anyone else, you should be free to do whatever the hell you want. The fact that you have to do these things in secret in most cases just shows how screwed up our current system is.

4. TRUST YOURSELF.

You are the only supreme power and authority in your life. Quit trusting your church spokesmen, politicians, corporate advertising, and other people's opinions and agenda for you. Don't even trust me! Trust the core of self that has gotten you this far in

life. Your intuitions, realizations, and solutions will
be the ones that are most right for you. Wake up to
those inner voices. Let them drown out the din of
the external chorus.

5. TAKE BOTH POWER AND RESPONSIBILITY FOR YOUR OWN LIFE.

Again, you are your own God. No one else can
change your life and make you happy. You have
to step up to the plate yourself. But you also have
the power to do so. All that is required is for you to
recognize it.

Accept that you are not an imperfect, infallible,
omnipotent god with power over everyone else, as
described in the Bible. Accept that you are perfect
in all your imperfections, just as you are. You have
the power to change things. But accepting that
power must also mean accepting the consequences
of your actions.

6. DARE TO BLAZE YOUR OWN PATH.

Don't be a follower. The well-beaten path just
leads the sheep to the slaughterhouse. Break from
the pack and run with the wolves, or run alone. I
guarantee that the paths you bushwhack yourself
through this jungle of a world will lead to much
better places.

Joseph Campbell calls this breaking from the
crowd "the left-hand path." This refers not to an evil
path, but simply to this: the old, traditional society
follows the right-hand path, working to conform
and follow those before them. New thought and
fresh perspective drives some, however, to turn and
walk away from the conservative path, to break

ground somewhere new and undiscovered.

It is not simply a turn in the opposite direction, but a spiralling out into new territory, a founding of a new approach. Break the circle we are trained to shuffle along forever, and forge your own path into the wilderness. When you look behind, you'll see a bright trail of Luciferian fire.

7. SPEAK UP WHEN THE TRUTH IS BEING MURDERED BY COWARDS.

You might be surprised just how powerful one voice can be against the tyranny, injustice and lies that bombard us from all sides. A properly worded letter to the editor can change a city. Speaking up for someone who cannot speak for themselves may change or even save a life. Calling the powers that be on their bullshit, pointing out that the Emperor has no clothes, questioning out loud the lies: these will transform our world.

In mythology, Satan dared to speak up against God's unilateral orders. Those who follow the Satanic path often have the courage to speak up against the lies, assumptions and tyranny of religion. Exercise your right to free speech whenever you have the chance. The more of us who do so, the more of us will be able to speak without fear of repression and persecution. The passionately spoken truth has far-reaching power.

8. LIVE IN THE PRESENT MOMENT.

There is no Heaven or Hell waiting for you at the end of your suffering, pious life. This moment is all you've got, and it won't come again. Our culture denies and hides death, but we all get it in the end.

Religion used our fear of death to concoct a brilliant and devious prison. The promise of eternal salvation, essentially eradicating death, is a lie that so many want desperately to believe, because what is more terrifying than one's own death?

Face your death and stare it right in the eye. Realize it is there waiting for you, like an old friend come to take you home. It is only then that you will begin to see how important each of your moments is.

Seize the day. The present moment is the only one in which you have any power. You can't change the past, and you can't predict the future. So take that moment and eke the most joy, effectiveness, and passion you can out of it!

9. DISCARD YOUR ASSUMPTIONS.

Certainly the assumptions made about Satanism are usually way off base. Take a lesson from this and challenge your own assumptions as they arise.

Approach things with an open mind. In Buddhism, this is often termed "child mind." Children have few assumptions. They are wired to learn from things-as-they-are, and their minds are insatiable. Become like them: curious and wide-eyed. Leave your preconceptions at the door, and your eyes will be clear enough to see the truth in all its messy glory.

10. ENJOY YOUR NATURAL URGES.

We are animals, wired to do animal things like eat, sleep, socialize, and have sex. We are also wired to celebrate, tell stories, change our consciousness, and let go and sing and dance around the fire. The fact that these things have been demonized for centuries does not change the fact that they are the core of us.

Imagine not only accepting these drives, but celebrating them. How much happier could we be if we could share erotic pleasure without shame? If we could recognize the sacred nature of our ordinary life, how much better would we feel about ourselves and our activities?

We are of the earth, of this corporeal world. Let us celebrate the gifts it has given us, those of pleasure, fun, joy, connection. In the Bible, a group of angels descended to earth in order to enjoy the wonders of this world, which surpassed that of heaven. Since heaven doesn't exist, this earth, this body, this way that we're built is all we've got. Better to enjoy it than to reject and rail against it for the rest of our life.

SATANIC SUPERPOWERS

Earlier, I said that being a Satanist doesn't grant you evil superpowers. I'm going to take a step back on that one. Being a Satanist actually does grant you some pretty amazing powers, though I wouldn't call them evil or even supernatural. I'm talking about the powers to make people think, to change minds, to dispel ignorance and even inspire others to live a happier life.

CHALLENGING ASSUMPTIONS

I am open about my Satanism. This forces new acquaintances, or old friends who just find out about my Satanism, to come to terms with any negative beliefs they may have about what Satanism means.

If you're raised in a Christian society, you are taught that Satanists are evil baby-sacrificing psychopaths, worshipping the Dark Lord in murderous bloody cults. However, most of the people I meet and befriend are of the smart, open-minded type. I am actually a pretty nice person. I guide my actions by Buddhist attitudes about compassion and kindness. I try to keep my word, and say what I mean and mean what I say. I like to make people laugh, and I like to cheer up my friends who are down. I don't hesitate to help those in need. I like to pay forward the generosity and compassion I've experienced in my own life.

My non-Satanic acquaintances have to reconcile the reality of who I am as a person with what they know about Satanism. It makes them re-examine those myths that were taught as unshakable truths by the religious establishment. They are forced to decide between two paradigms: Satanist as evil babykiller, or Satanist as an ordinary, kind person. I am pleased to report that I have lost very few friends due to my "coming out" as a Satanist.

Some of them have even asked me questions about it — real, respectful questions without pre-judgement. I'm not trying to "convert" anyone with my Satanism, but I do enjoy making people think and potentially question the dominant paradigm that they've unknowingly internalized.

It's the beginning of a line of questioning that can lead to vast sea changes in society itself. When you realize that the myth of the evil Satanist is just a myth, you might turn your critical eyes to other myths perpetuated by our Christian-dominated culture and start questioning them too. The myth that women are inferior. That gays are evil. That you must burn in hell for your questioning. If you have your eyes opened to the untruth of such a basic pre-sumption — that Satanists must be evil, since Satan is — you might realize that the entire system based on that presumption is flawed.

As a Satanist, you have great powers to create cognitive dissonance:

> "The term cognitive dissonance is used to describe the feeling of discomfort that results from holding two conflicting beliefs. When there is a discrepancy between beliefs and behaviors, something must change in order to eliminate or reduce the dissonance." [4]

When someone comes face to face with an articulate, rational, compassionate Satanist, any blind faith they may have in Christian notions of good (God) and evil (Satan) must come into question. Now they have two competing beliefs in their head, and they must discard or disbelieve one of them to resolve that uncomfortable, "my head doesn't make sense" feeling.

In many cases, religious nuts will refuse to acknowledge any new information or experience that conflicts with their core God beliefs. They will see a Satanist as evil no matter what.

I don't think we are ever going to change these people's minds. All the myriad proofs of modern science can't convince these people that evolution is real; why would they accept the fact that a Satanist isn't actually out to rape, kill and eat their children?

But we do have the power to drastically enlighten other people — the non-nuts, the reasonable ones, the ones who actually want to think for themselves. Our very existence sows the seed of doubt in a heart not shuttered tight against the truth.

And our intelligent discourse with those who want to engage us can change the minds of those around us who watch that debate. There is something about simply being a Satanist that calls up the most angry, ignorant, blustery responses from close-minded Christians. When that happens, the people watching get to see the true colors of bigotry fly, and many of them end up disgusted, turning away from supporting the bigots.

We all have that power to cause cognitive dissonance, should we choose to use it. To reconcile two conflicting beliefs, you must discard one of them. Sometimes the truth wins, if it is demonstrated clearly enough and falls on a open, rational mind.

THE EMPEROR HAS NO CLOTHES

Satanism points out the hypocrisies in Christian actions like no other path. You can think of this as the power to point out that the emperor has no clothes.

Some in the Christian church cry "religious freedom" in order to ram its beliefs down the throats of every American citizen. If you cry religious freedom and pass legislation allowing Christianity in public government, schools and other civic organizations, Christians, then you must also let us insert our own practices and beliefs into the mix. If you want to mix Church and state, you'll also have to let Satanists in.

The Satanic Temple exploits this hypocrisy to fight for the separation of church and state in highly public ways. They've petitioned to place a large statue of Baphomet on the same Oklahoma Capitol lawn as an existing Ten Commandments monument. When a Florida court ruled that public schools that allow Christians to distribute literature to kids must allow all faiths to do so, the Satanic Temple responded by creating a "Satanic Kids' Activity Book" for distribution, which actually teaches tolerance and acceptance.

These cases bring out the best and worst in people: invariably there is hypocritical knee-jerk bashing from at least one religious nut, showing the ugly side to the watching public, especially in contrast to the reasonable request for equal religious freedom made by the Satanist. Across the nation, scholars, legal experts and even some of those who consider themselves Christian are now rallying behind the Satanic Temple, commenting that the Satanists are showing far more Christian principles than the so-called Christian religious leaders.

Hearts open. Minds change. Tolerance grows. Simply by being a Satanist, you are subverting the dominant paradigm, and if you are open about it in any way, your superpowers increase exponentially.

The downside to being an open Satanist is that you set yourself up for attack and discrimination. I am lucky to have built a life where I don't have to worry about losing my job or kids over my Satanism. Not everyone has that luxury.

But let me conclude with one more Satanic superpower: the power to make people leave you alone. If you're ignorant enough to believe that I am in league with the actual Devil, you probably believe that I have the power of evil enchantment, or at least the will to do really terrible things to you should you get on my bad side. That's fine by me. That self-selects you right out of my circle of acquaintances and I won't have to engage in constant, pointless debate with the intolerant.

Being openly Satanist is like having a strong social filter set to "on." If someone can't deal with it, they will go out of their way to avoid you. And I like that. It saves me the trouble of dealing with intolerance and idiocy much of the time.

THE SATANIC RECOVERY ALTERNATIVE

Addiction dogged me the majority of my adult life. I spent 17 years addicted to huffing nitrous oxide, a year and half addicted to meth, and five months addicted to heroin. I'm happy to report I've been clean for over a year now, and I feel confident I've left addiction behind.

In every case, I quit on my own. But first I wasted years trying to get clean in twelve step programs, which actually hindered my recovery instead of helping. In these programs, the core belief is you cannot stop using drugs; you have to let God do it for you. This approach drove back to addiction again and again.

I believe it's time to move to a more effective, science-based model of treating addiction, one that doesn't rely on an external power to heal. I believe it's time we put our efforts into mental health care, social justice and universal access to proven treatments instead of leaving recovery up to these twelve-step groups. I believe it's time we recognize our own power to make the deepest changes in our life.

THE FEEDBACK LOOP OF DEPRESSION AND ADDICTION

My family suffers from severe clinical depression, and I'm no exception. For the first 41 years of my life, I operated with a broken mind. I was constantly thinking about suicide, and I was a frequent self-harmer, bashing my head on walls, biting myself, throwing myself in front of traffic.

My depression latched onto addiction as soon as I entered college. First I became a binge drinker. Then from the time I was 22 until I was 39, I was increas-

ingly addicted to huffing nitrous oxide — "whip-its."
People told me nitrous is not a real drug, and I
didn't have an addiction. But I knew better. By the
time I was 28, I understood that I had a major drug
problem. I would easily spend $3000 or more a
month buying whipped cream canisters, huffing 600
or more at a time without stopping for days, until I
ran out of money. I did not not eat or sleep as long
as there was nitrous left.

I was depriving my brain of oxygen for extended
periods of time. I'd end up in the hospital, dazed,
dehydrated and suicidal. I could feel the brain damage, yet I kept going. I actually wanted to kill my
brain and my intelligence, because they had only
brought me pain.

I lost my $400,000 home, my well-paying con-
sulting jobs, my partner and my friends. And I lost
any shred of self-esteem and self-compassion that
I might have harbored. It was full steam ahead on
the path of self-destruction, and I couldn't get off
the train.

TRYING TO QUIT

I wanted so badly to be free of the addiction. I
willed myself over and over again to never go back
to the drugs again, but when the urge hit me, it
was like I became possessed. The depression grew
because no matter what I did, no matter how hard I
tried, I could not shake the addiction. Depression fed
the addiction, and the addiction fed the depression.

After trying to quit on my own for several years,
I was told by my boyfriend to join the twelve-step
program Narcotics Anonymous (NA). I was desperate to try anything that might help me fight the

addiction that was destroying my life.

I tried for years to use the tools NA gave me to fight the addiction. Going to meetings at least three days a week, getting a sponsor, working the steps — I was hungry for recovery, and everyone in the rooms talked about it like a promised land. I put my all into the program. It was great getting the support from others who knew all too well what drug addiction was like. These people genuinely wanted to help me. Their stories gave me hope.

But I almost immediately spotted a problem, a huge incompatibility with my core philosophy.

These (below) are twelve steps of the program. They are the same steps as in Alcoholics Anonymous, Overeaters Anonymous, Gamblers Anonymous and all other twelve step programs. You are expected to write long, detailed essays on each of these steps and work with a sponsor to fully understand and internalize these steps. You are also directed to pray on them.

THE 12 STEPS OF NARCOTICS ANONYMOUS

1. We admitted that we were powerless over our addiction, that our lives had become unmanageable.
2. We came to believe that a Power greater than ourselves could restore us to sanity.
3. We made a decision to turn our will and our lives over to the care of God as we understood Him.
4. We made a searching and fearless moral inventory of ourselves.
5. We admitted to God, to ourselves, and to another human being the exact nature of our wrongs.
6. We were entirely ready to have God remove all these defects of character.

7. We humbly asked Him to remove our short-comings.
8. We made a list of all persons we had harmed, and became willing to make amends to them all.
9. We made direct amends to such people wherever possible, except when to do so would injure them or others.
10. We continued to take personal inventory, and when we were wrong promptly admitted it.
11. We sought through prayer and meditation to improve our conscious contact with God as we understood Him, praying only for knowledge of His will for us and the power to carry that out.
12. Having had a spiritual awakening as a result of these steps, we tried to carry this message to addicts, and to practice these principles in all our affairs. [5]

God plays the key role in these steps. In all twelve step programs, the core belief is that only something outside you can take away your addiction. Once you've found your higher power, you admit you are powerless and can't fix your problem yourself, so you turn it over to God and pray for him to remove your "defects of character." Your higher power, your God, is the only one who will save you, fix your defects, bring you back to sanity, and all the other necessary work that you yourself are incapable of doing. You are free to choose anything as your higher power — except yourself.

I hadn't yet found Satanism at the time, but as a magician, I held my true will as the highest power in my life. This belief in my own power formed the core of my reality, just as it does in Satanism — you are your own God.

But in NA, I was told that your higher power can be anything except yourself. I specifically asked about the self as higher power, since that is my path as a magician. I was told in no uncertain terms, "that is the one thing your higher power cannot be." It can be God, a Goddess, Buddha, the NA group itself, "or even a doorknob," as my sponsor said. But it absolutely cannot be your self.

As an atheist and magician, I had a great deal of difficulty accepting this model. But I tried hard to follow it, since I was told that was the only way to stop the addiction.

But it backfired. Instead, giving up my core belief and turning everything over to some other power drove me back to the drugs again and again. By accepting that I was powerless, I was in fact rendered powerless. In other words, when I got the nitrous craving, I said to myself, "I am powerless to stop this addiction. I can't help it. So here I go to buy the nitrous!"

I have no concept of an external power — not God, not even nature or the NA group itself — that would reach in and stop me. I have no such belief, no matter how hard I try to muster one. I had lived my life seeking the power of my true will; now I had to discard that path.

In fact, NA specifically attacks the will, warning you against following it. There was a man in my group whose derogatory nickname was "Self-Will Bill." He sheepishly admitted that he was known for following his own will way too often instead of

God's. The belief is that our own will is flawed, and we must give up all choice and will to God instead, praying constantly to determine what his will is instead of ours.

I could have actively sought out clinical treatment for my depression, but NA (at least the groups I was in) was against psychological medications. In the groups I was in, they considered antidepressants to be drugs in the same class as coke and heroin ("they change your consciousness!").

They shamed one poor group member there into going off his meds, despite his severe mental illness. His girlfriend left him and he hung himself from his rafters soon after.

By the end of my addiction and my time in NA, I was worse than ever, and I saw no way out, because I had drunk the Kool-aid and believed I was indeed powerless. I saw myself as a weak, broken addict who would never be able to quit. I had no higher power that would fix me, and I was told again and again that I could never do it myself. I resigned myself to a long, slow, hellish suicide with drugs for the rest of my life.

FINDING SOMETHING BETTER

But then something unexpected happened. I met my husband and fell in love, and suddenly there was something worth fighting for, something that brought me real joy instead of a quick fix.

My husband is a Satanist, and he loved me with total acceptance and without judgment. His gentle but strong belief in me restored me to my own power again. One day soon after we started seeing each other, I woke up and left the nitrous behind. I had realized nitrous was getting in the way of our fantastic sex. There was no contest; I didn't even crave the nitrous again after setting it down. I chose real pleasure instead of the false promises of the drug.

COPING WITH HELL

This pattern repeated itself twice more. Once my husband and I got together, our world fell apart around us. We left our partners and had nowhere to live. We tried moving to the San Francisco Bay Area, but twice in a row dishonest landlords dumped us on the street overnight, and we became homeless.

It was sheer hell. I was unable to get my Paxil (antidepressant) prescription. I went clinically insane and suicidal. After many hopeless months of searching for housing, we were still without a stable home. We turned to meth as a desperate attempt to cope with what was an unbearable situation. Though it was far from an ideal solution, it kept me from committing suicide in the face of insurmountable odds.

Finally, after a year of running from one emergency housing situation to the next, a friend paid the deposit on an apartment for us in Seattle. At last, I had a place to work again. Our life stabilized, and we were no longer living in crushing fear and despair. Within a month of moving into our own place, we stopped using meth and never went back.

BEATING HEROIN

I worked hard over the next two years. The massage work I was doing is extremely physical, and I was already injured from several falls during the homeless period. My back and knees started to go out with severe arthritis. I couldn't work through the intense, constant pain.

A doctor prescribed opiate pain pills, which allowed me to work. But there was a price. I got addicted to the pills, and once you're strung out on opiates, it is near impossible to quit because the withdrawals are worse than death itself.

When my prescription ran out, I turned to street heroin. Within five months of starting, I had developed a $100/day heroin habit. I dripped it down my nose every two hours and still felt like hell, because it had stopped working for the pain. I was just taking it not to get sick.

By two months in, I was horrified by how this addiction had snuck up on me. I needed off the drugs ASAP, and as a Satanist I knew nobody could make it happen but me. I immediately got to work on trying to find help. I called every detox program in Seattle, but they were all full.

I knew there was a prescription drug formulated specifically to prevent withdrawal symptoms — Suboxone, or buprenorphine as it known generically. This drug can stop opiate or heroin addiction cold turkey, with no bad side effects. If it were readily available, we would have far less opiate addicts, because almost all of us want to stop but can't because of the withdrawals.

But the big pharma companies don't want people to get off their very profitable pain pills, and they pull the strings in Washington. They convinced the federal government to restrict buprenorphine, allowing only a few doctors to have a license to prescribe it. The license is extremely expensive, so only the richest private doctors can afford it, and they charge exorbitant rates for treatment and don't take Medicare or Medicaid. We could not afford it.

We were lucky. A friend was able to get us some buprenorphine on the black market. We were able to quit heroin completely over the course of just 8 days, with no withdrawals except some anxiety. I credit friendship and compassion for saving our lives once again.

After getting off the heroin, I realized that I had to make a massive effort to build a life with no room for drugs. My Satanic principles taught me that only I could make the changes needed to avoid any future addiction traps. I set out determined to become the person I was always meant to be, so strong and secure in myself that I would not fall prey to the drugs again.

I threw myself full tilt into finishing the BDSM instructional video I was working on, as well as reaching out and building new friendships, becoming physically active, and doing whatever it took to reach the life I wanted.

I took the initiative on finding the right mental health care for my ongoing depression. I finally found the right psych med, buproprion (Welbutrin), and was amazed at how my brain righted itself almost immediately. It proved without a doubt that my brain chemicals had been the source of my crushing depression all along.

A BETTER SYSTEM

My story shows that the traditional twelve step recovery programs are not the only option for addicts desperate to quit. If I had found the right mental health care early on, I might have steered clear of the maelstrom of depression and addiction in the first place. If there had been social services available to help me find housing right away, I would never have turned to the meth. And if I had believed in myself all those long years instead of trying to believe in God's wisdom and grace, I might have taken the steps to rebuild my life without the drugs long ago.

In the end, it was my Satanic belief that only I could fix the problem that led me to solutions. In every case, the solution was finding something better than the drug, something that gave me more joy and pleasure — my lover, a stable place to live, compassionate friends, and finally healing my broken mind and unlocking the potential that lay inside me all this time.

If we want to offer real recovery as a society, we need to think outside the twelve-step box and make a real commitment to helping addicts recover under their own power.

For a list of resources to help with recovery, see page 128.

FEAR VS. COMPASSION

I see two clear paths set before me in my own interactions with other humans, and I believe this dichotomy lies at the heart of much of our human world. My shorthand for these two directions is fear vs. compassion. Satanism has played a key role for me both in overcoming fear and finally being able to give myself the compassion I need and deserve.

THE PATH OF FEAR

It's easy to see where the path of fear leads, because all you have to do is look at today's world. We live in a world built by fear, buttressed with lies and violence. We are trained from birth to be good God-fearing sheeple, to fear everything that is different or new. Our fear makes us easy to control.

Fear is bred by those in power, those terribly afraid of any threat to their rule, and harnessed effectively in multiple channels to keep us under their thumb.

Religion sets up a straw man for us to fear in Satan. Government sets up enemies and terrorists for us to fear so we agree to give up our rights without complaint. The news bombards us with constant reasons to fear for ourselves, our children, our safety. And the mass-market culture teaches us to fear not being good enough because we don't have the latest phone, most expensive anti-wrinkle cream, largest car, newest diet pill.

From the gate, we are also taught to fear ourselves. Supposedly, our sinful nature lies ever in wait, ready to overwhelm us with evil thoughts and deeds. We are taught to reject anything in us that does not conform or obey and learn to just mouth the words along with the rest of the herd. The herd mentality tells us that if we do not conform, the predator will single us out.

I see fear at the root of all the wrongs humans perpetuate upon each other. If you are afraid of someone because they are different, you will have no problem hurting or killing them. Animals lash out in fear, and humans are just another animal.

We lie out of fear, we bully and abuse because of our fearful insecurities, and we perpetuate grand genocides out of the fear of the "other." Women are caged, cloaked, suppressed, tightly owned and controlled because religion fears the supposed all-destroying power of their sexuality. We are taught to fear our own natural sexual and animal urges and we are taught to fear pleasure, because only suffering is virtuous. And our resulting unhappiness makes us eager to swallow the false promises of priests, politicians and commercials.

We keep quiet in the face of injustice, because we are afraid of retaliation. Even in our daily life, we cling to soul-killing jobs we hate to buy things we don't need because we are afraid of the unknown alternatives.

THE TURN AWAY FROM FEAR

If you have arrived at Satanism, then you have already made a tremendously courageous step. Choosing to check out these ideas is a turn away from fear. What could take more guts than to declare yourself affiliated with Satan, the being the Big Three Monotheisms consider to be the most evil force in the universe, the direct enemy of God?

LaVey himself called Satanism "The Feared Religion." We know that those who fear something will often try to destroy it. To say you are opening yourself up to persecution by choosing to become a Satanist is an understatement. The fact that you are willing to take that risk for an idea alone means you do not let fear dictate your choices and actions in life. You have already learned not to listen to fear.

ACCEPTING FEAR

The turn away from fear is not so much the denial, suppression or elimination of fear so much as the choice not to let the fear guide your choices. The fear will be there, no matter what. Real bravery is not the lack of fear, but rather the courage to move ahead anyway despite the fear. The more crippling the fear, the greater the bravery — and in my experience, the greater the reward.

Everything I've achieved in life, I've done through facing my fear squarely, admitting it, and choosing to go forward regardless of the shrill screaming voices in my head. I succeeded in the corporate world because of my ability to take intelligently-managed risks.

The stable and meaningful life I live now only came about because I've decided to tackle seemingly insurmountable odds over and over again. You might be surprised at your own strength and capabilities when you move past fear.

FINDING COMPASSION

I believe that the turn away from fear is a turn towards compassion. Many sources in my life have shown me that the highest good among humans is compassion. Not pity, not self-sacrifice, but the simple acknowledgement that another being is like you inside and wants to be free from suffering.

My Buddhist background holds compassion at its heart. Buddhist teachings point the practitioner to a compassionate approach to the world. Those who wish to go the extra mile and become Bodhisattvas, living incarnations of enlightened beings, make four vows, the first two of which are:

I vow to rescue the boundless living beings from suffering.

I vow to put an end to the infinite afflictions of living beings.

The Bodhisattva path is not for everyone, not even me, but it says a lot that the highest ideal of this spiritual path is not obedience (as in Christianity), but rather compassion and the ending of suffering. This seems like a much more practical approach to me, one that would result in more happiness and less suffering all around.

PERSONAL EXPERIENCE

In the last four years of crisis, destruction and rebirth in my personal life, it was human compassion that saved my life time and time again. Not the current system, not God, not even hard work and perseverance on my part could overcome some of the challenges I faced. It was the help of friends old and new that picked me and my husband up out of the gutter when we had nothing to grab ahold of.

Without that compassion, we would be dead

several times over. The help we got, unasked for and from people already struggling in their own life, saved us from suicide and gave us the leg up we needed to build our own strong, stable life. I've seen human compassion work real miracles when all hope was lost.

SATANISM AND SELF-COMPASSION

Compassion must begin with self-compassion, and that is where I see Satanism stepping in. You must have compassion for yourself just as you are, in all your supposed sin and flaws and shortfallings. You are doing the best you can in an insane, dysfunctional world. And there is nothing wrong with you, despite the fearful shrill voices of that world yelling at you that there is.

You are a complete, organic being with many dimensions, and you have the ultimate power to change your own life and world experience. In other words, you are your own God. I believe this to be the core message of Satanism.

When you act with compassion towards yourself, you will find times when you cannot help others because it would harm or drain you. But when you practice compassion for and acceptance of yourself in all your ups and downs, you'll find that friendship and connection will flow more easily in your life, and your compassion will start spilling over in wonderful, collaborative ways.

The path away from fear leads not only towards compassion, but also to simply passion. When you aren't hampered by fear, the sky's the limits to your dreams. Passion will drive you through the world in a sweet fire if you let it. Don't fear the burn.

"PASSION WITH"

To me, the word compassion also conjures up its component parts: "com" (with, together); and "passion." By tapping deep into both your compassion and passion despite fear, you are putting yourself in a space to receive the wondrous and life-changing gift of "passion-with."

In other words, you will find yourself more likely to stumble upon shared passions with other amazing folks who have given the finger to fear. This spark of shared passion can transcend the sum of the parts and create a larger, inspired, communal whole that leads you and your companions to revolutionary, creative, joyful paths, and to the happiness that comes from finally knowing you are not alone.

FACING THE ONCOMING STORM

This week, yet another climate change report came out, detailing the changes that are already in full swing, significantly changing our environment. We've set in motion a positive feedback loop that can't be stopped, only survived. I believe that as a race, we've reached a fork in the road: we either make drastic changes to work together, or we face our own extinction.

We have passed the point of no return, when the changes we've wrought on this planet are now unstoppable. If we are to survive the ever-increasing danger of our own environment, we must pull together like never before and work as one united community. We'll need to transcend our fear of each other and realize that our "tribe" is now everyone on this planet. Otherwise the few who do survive will be the .01% at the top, leaving the rest of humanity to suffer and die.

EVER-GREATER EXTREMES

A recent report released by the National Climate Assessment calls out what is already happening:

> "Certain types of extreme weather events with links to climate change have become more frequent and/or intense, including prolonged periods of heat, heavy downpours, and, in some regions, floods and droughts. In addition, warming is causing sea level to rise and glaciers and Arctic sea ice to melt, and oceans are becoming more acidic as they absorb carbon dioxide. These and other aspects of climate change are disrupting people's lives and damaging some sectors of our economy."[6]

The executive editor of Scientific American, Frank Guterl, recently published a book titled "The Fate of the Species: Why the Human Race May Cause Its Own Extinction and How We Can Stop It." Scientists agree that we have passed the point at which we can reverse the devastation we've done to our environment, particularly our weather and climate systems. Even if we pulled together now and miraculously cut our carbon emissions in half, we still wouldn't be able to stop the process, only slow it down a little. We must begin bracing for impact as our weather spirals farther and farther into extremes.

THE ENERGY CRISIS

Even without climate change, we are facing a huge cliff: the end of oil. Renewable resources are being developed, but at nowhere near the rate needed to satisfy the insatiable energy needs of this world once it uses up all its oil. It's not just your personal auto freedom that's at stake: electricity, food transport, even research itself all depends on energy that in most countries is anything but renewable.

It's more than a brownout in New York. It's food not making it to the city from the farm. It's communications breaking down. It's a house of cards that we've built on endless oil, and when that card is pulled, the whole thing can come crashing down overnight.

The good news is Europe has taken the lead in developing wind, solar, wave and other power. We might just be able to break our oil addiction after all. In 2014, over 40% of Germany's power came from solar and renewables, for instance, and China is rapidly developing its solar farms.

If we pulled together globally, we might be able to make the jump to solar before our infrastructure collapses. With cheap and plentiful energy from solar, we would have a much better chance of surviving the coming climate apocalypse. Solar could provide energy for irrigating deserts, transporting people out of the many coastal cities that will be flooded, powering desalinators, and much more, all without raising our carbon emissions. But the key is that we have to put all our strength and cooperation into it right now, and so far our response has been far too sluggish.

SWIFT AND SUDDEN CHAOS

Modern society does a good job of completely insulating us from the harsh realities of the world: hunger, cold, fighting, death. Tell your average American that the microwave is broken and you'll get the blank terror of "but what will we eat?" If our comfortably insulated world breaks down, it's not going to be pretty.

In industrialized nations, most of the population would find itself completely unprepared for survival in anything but the cushiest world.

Most of us have absolutely no clue how close we are to having our worlds destroyed. I didn't know it myself until it happened to me: losing my housing twice in a short period through no fault of my own, suddenly I was homeless and living on the streets, relegated to the trash bin of society. It happened without warning, and once down there I would have had no way to get back up into housing and a job without the help of very generous friends. You don't realize that your house is built on sand until it washes away in the storm.

I wish I could trust in the compassion that is basic to our human nature, but I've seen far too much. If compassion means rethinking your beliefs, changing your preconceptions, or simply inconveniencing you in some small way, it's too much for Westerners. We are raised in a cesspool of suspicion and fear, where the hungry and poor are perceived as immoral monsters out to steal your hard-earned goods.

And history plays out all over the world in the same ways: the voices of reason and compassion are crushed under the juggernaut of unending war, killing, rape, injustice, oppression and overwhelming greed. We have to make major changes to stop this tide.

THE DISSOLUTION OF MASS MEDIA

We can no longer trust the media to give us the real story. In fact, mass media is dying an ever-quickening death. All that's left is a hollow shell. News and information has decentralized, and that's a good thing. It's now up to us to connect, to share our personal stories and initiate real discussion on the issues that are staring us in the face. There won't be help from anyone, especially not the media.

A CONVENIENT FALLACY

The root of much of our dysfunction lies in our inability to see others as actual human beings, like us. All you have to do is look around you to see the suffering inflicted on one human being by another. Compassion may be our birthright, but ignorance, hate, fear and violence are what we choose time and time again.

When we grow with self-hate planted in our heart from the beginning by the Church, by parents, by peers or societal pressures, it is no wonder that we blossom into agents of our own destruction. We've been programmed too well. We are taught to fear the other, to fear new ideas and change. Only fear and loneliness can keep us good little sheeple, easily controlled and plundered for our resources. No wonder this hate so often bubbles up in horrific ways.

I admit I was blind to this dysfunction until I became homeless. Suddenly, through no fault of my own, I became human excrement to those still in the normal world. I was treated worse than a cockroach. My struggle for basic survival — food, shelter from the rain, a place to sleep — was seen as a direct attack on human civilization. I was driven from place to place with such derision and hate that after three days I decided to end it all and commit suicide. It was obvious the world wanted me to not exist.

If it were only a matter of physical survival, I could have made it. But I couldn't handle the psychological trauma of instantly becoming the most hated being on the planet. I was bewildered by how I was treated, as if I were a murderer or worse instead of a victim of really awful circumstances.

Later I found an explanation: instead of acting with compassion when confronted with the monumental tragedies (like homelessness) our system creates, we try to make ourselves feel better by blaming the victims. This is based on something called the just-world fallacy, a fallacy encouraged and spread by religions that claim everything is the result of God's will, no matter how awful it is.

> "The just-world hypothesis (or just-world fallacy) is the cognitive bias that human actions eventually yield morally fair and fitting consequences, so that, ultimately, noble actions are duly rewarded and evil actions are duly punished. In other words, the just-world hypothesis is the tendency to attribute consequences to, or expect consequences as the result of, an unspecified power that restores moral balance; the fallacy is that this implies the existence of such a power in terms of some cosmic force of justice, desert, stability, or order in the universe." [7]

More recently, researchers have explored how people react to poverty through the lens of the just world hypothesis. The results of their studies?

> "High belief in a just world is associated with blaming the poor, and low belief in a just world is associated with identifying external causes of poverty including world economic systems, war, and exploitation." [8]

In other words, if we aren't blinded by the fallacy that God meant for the person to suffer, we might actually go about fixing the problems that cause the suffering. But it's more convenient to think the person did something to bring their terrible suffering upon themselves. This gets rid of our guilt.

In rape cases, this is often called "victim blaming." But blaming the victim seems to be a favorite pastime in all situations. It helps explain why as a suffering homeless person I was treated like a filthy rat who needed to be stamped out, not a human being in dire need of basic survival.

We must move beyond this just-world misconception if we are to work together to truly survive as a species.

TIME TO CONNECT

So what can we do? If we have any hope for future generations, then we must transcend our outdated models and begin actively building new systems — together. The rise of the Internet has given us the tools we need to connect. We can work together outside of the existing government and corporate structures. We can drop our ridiculous anti-science religious leaders and embrace technology, understand what is actually happening, and put our all into developing solutions as fast as possible.

I believe the first step is simple: end our isolation. Drop our masks, reach out to others, dare to show our true colors and share our real stories. We have the capacity for great compassion and great positive change. I believe if we connect over the vast global net, change will come as we realize we are all just people, people who deserve compassion and help and understanding just as we do.

I believe this will come not from top-down organization or authority, but instead from the bottom up as we share our personal stories with each other. Sharing your story helps others see the human in you. Reaching out to others builds friendship and understanding, the connecting glue that can hold us together in the face of the massive ordeals sweeping toward us.

The storm has just begun. We have time to save our race, but not much. The stakes are too high to remain paralyzed by fear and hate. As a species, we must choose now between connection and certain death. Let us reach out and connect across the globe and share our real stories, our fears, our pain, our joys. If we can break through the isolation, we can begin building the new models that will sustain us in the darkest times ahead. If we can't, then I honestly can't see much hope for humanity.

BUSTING THE GENDER DUALITY MYTH

Many Satanists use the goat-headed image of Baphomet as their sacred emblem. In Eli Levy's influential drawing of Baphomet, he is seen with both male and female characteristics, integrating both in one sacred hermaphroditic being. This is symbolic of the non-dualistic nature of Satanism: that is, we reject the dichotomy of God vs. Satan and instead work with something completely different: our own divinity.

The narrowly dualistic mindset encouraged by Christianity hampers growth, freedom and progress wherever it has taken hold. We need to question every duality, and I believe one of the most important to take on is the duality of gender and the idea that one is superior to the other. I believe if we observe ourselves and the world, we will find that inside we are not so different, despite owning different genitals. Baphomet contains both male and female, yin and yang. Like him, we are integrated beings, not defined by or reduced to our gender.

WORKING TOGETHER

It was to the Church's benefit, as well as the political powers, to keep the sexes separate and at war with each other so they wouldn't have a moment of clarity and realize that if they worked together, they could stand up to their overlords.

I believe both men and women will have to work together to change ingrained systems of discrimination, persecution and rape that have come out of centuries of sexism and abuse. I believe that it is to the advantage of everyone in a society to end discrimination of any kind. How much farther would we be along the curve of scientific progress or technology if more women felt comfortable going into math and science, for instance? The solution to surviving global warming could be locked in the mind of a poor black girl in Africa.

Any woman who submits herself to any of the Big Three Monotheisms is, in my view, either insane, idiotic, or has no choice, forced into it by her family or culture. In the monotheistic worldview, women are supposedly the root of all evil. Men are taught to avoid their natural sexual attraction to women and view it as the Devil's temptation or black sorcery.

No wonder our society is so screwed up when it comes to treating men and women differently. We all need to set aside the bullshit and just treat each other like human beings. Satanism doesn't stipulate that one sex or the other is divine; each of us as individuals, regardless of our physical attributes, are our own god. That goes for both women and men.

DESTROYING THE STEREOTYPES WITH SCIENCE

Science has recently proven beyond a doubt that, apart from the obvious physical ones (height, shoulder to hip ratio, genitals), there is actually very little difference between the sexes.

I've felt this non-gendered consciousness strongly all my life. I've gone through life, as one friend puts it, "as a man," despite my busty female form. I have never been conscious of being female, except when someone is reacting to my feminine sexuality. It's not something that I'm aware of most of the time. I have many friends, male, female, trans and genderqueer, who report the same thing.

A recent study by Harry Reis and Bobbi Carothers, published in the February 2012 issue of the Journal of Personality and Social Psychology, confirmed this hunch: in almost all ways save a few physical characteristics, men and women aren't statistically different. The psychological differences between individuals are far greater than between men and women, and it's impossible to predict gender from psychological responses.

This is a large-scale study that compiled data from multiple studies on over 13,000 individuals and looked at 122 different characteristics:

> *"The researchers ... concluded that characteristics that we traditionally associate with one sex or the other actually exist on a continuum. There are not two distinct genders, but instead there are linear gradations of variables associated with sex, such as masculinity or intimacy, all of which are continuous." [9]*

All our constant speculation about innate differences between men vs. women is thus for naught. There is no such thing as a "manly man" and a "girly girl." All the stereotypes about male vs. female personalities are false.

Some of us may be so free of societal gender constraints that we flow fluidly through gender identities, as hermaphroditic as Baphomet, integrating both female and male into one, refusing to be pigeon-holed into one rigid box. I have had the pleasure of befriending many genderqueer individuals, young and old, who are brave enough to stand up to the imposed division and be whole just as they are. They inspire me in my own search for integration and wholeness.

Don't buy into the fear pushed by the system, trying to load you with false judgements about each gender. And don't repress the portions of yourself that don't fit neatly into your gender stereotype. Move beyond the duality. We have all of us yin and yang inside us. May the wisdom of Baphomet inspire us to work together to transcend these false dualistic divisions.

INCENDIARY BREASTS

I was recently banned from using my social media platform (Facebook) for three days because I posted a piece of art that included the female breast. It made me angry, because Facebook is my social support network, and I had just founded a chronic pain support group; now I was cut off from my network of support. Censorship strikes again, protecting us from phantom dangers by taking away our rights to communicate and express ourselves.

Censorship of our personal expression is rampant, justified by fearful corporate concerns for the bottom line. And we have no recourse, because indeed, Facebook is a company and not an open public forum, and we agree to abide by their rules when we use their free service. I can't argue with that. But I can argue with the ridiculous beliefs and attitudes that form the very root of this drive to censorship, because they are all based on cowardice, shame and fear.

WHY CENSORSHIP?

Satanism has a proud tradition of defying censors, just by its existence. Let us take Satan's lead and question the authorities: Why is censorship necessary?

I could write volumes about censorship in general, including the sorry state of our news media, suppression of journalism, and the government/corporate control of our information flow. But this week, I'd like to single out the censorship of nudity and sexuality.

AN INDECENT PROPOSAL

Why did my art post freak the Facebook prudes out so much? I see plenty of frankly pornographic boob images go through my feed daily, with pasties or other nipple covers. But if you can actually see the dot that represents the nipple, it becomes a dangerous image that might offend investors — er, I mean users.

Let's take a cold hard look at "decency" standards. This assumes that the naked nipple is indecent, as is the naked cock or cunt. The fear is that a child will see an image of the naked body and be forever scarred. Or the child might encounter sexuality and ask their parents questions the parents are too ashamed to answer.

This strikes me as an incredible assumption on the part of the powers that be: the assumption that there is something fundamentally wrong with sexuality and nudity, that they are shameful and damaging to minds old and young alike. That protecting our young from knowledge about a fundamental part of themselves will serve them well in the long run. That if the naked female breast was given the same rights as the male one, society would collapse.

This assumption is part and parcel of our Christian history and the Puritanical roots of our society. It is the assumption that supports the campaign of shame the father-god religions wage against their followers to keep them meekly repentant and easily controlled.

FEAR THE BOOBIES

Women are hit particularly hard by this campaign, because our sexuality is considered inherently sinful. It is generally accepted that men are sexual beings, even though the Church tries to pour as much shame as possible onto them as well. Women are expected to be completely nonsexual, and any who develop a libido or joy in the pleasures of their body are branded dangerous sluts. The naked female breast is a symbol of dangerous feminine sexuality to the censors, whether or not it actually represents that to the viewer or to the woman who owns it.

Here is my view on the matter: the censors are afraid of the boobies. The censors are a consortium of bitter, impotent dried-up men who are terrified of their own sexual response. Desire and lust can feel overpowering, especially to those who deny and repress those feelings on a regular basis. Since the inception of the father-god hierarchical religious tyranny, a woman's body was assigned a highly dangerous power, that of awakening sexual feelings in a man.

So the woman's body was controlled, covered, owned, sold. Her own sexuality was stamped out in an effort to control the arousal such a sexuality could inspire in men. Boobies became dangerous. Accidentally seeing one could turn you into a lust-crazed monster (see also: viewing an ankle in Victorian times; seeing a woman's bare face in militant Islamic cultures). Boobs are everywhere, in our face, selling us everything from beer to cars. But seeing an actual nipple: unholiest of unholies!

America lives in a complete state of sexual denial, and it's a legacy of our Puritanical foundations, one unfairly imposed on those of us with more progressive, natural, scientific views about sexuality and nudity.

BUT WHAT ABOUT THE CHILDREN?

I'm going to put forth a shocking argument here: seeing and learning about nudity and sexuality at a young age is not damaging to the developing mind. In fact, it's anything but! I believe it is the lack of education about sex and our bodies that cause the most damage.

Let's take myself as an example. I grew up in an environment where nudity and sex was natural and not hidden. I was raised by hippies in the woods. My parents walked around naked all the time. I could hear them having sex in our small cabin. When I was seven, my parents went to the library and checked me out an educational book on sex. It was very scientific and contained plenty of graphic illustrations.

At 14, I decided I wanted to have sex with my long-term boyfriend. My mom took me to Planned Parenthood and held my hand during the exam. Later I helped girl friends with less progressive parents through the same process. Several of them later thanked me for helping them avoid teen pregnancy.

I've worked in the sex industry as a BDSM educator, dominatrix and an erotic masseuse for many years, and have always had good experiences. My sexuality is my own, and I can choose to use it however I like. I've helped many people find the intimacy and joy they were searching for.

I have brought many of my female friends to women-owned sex shops and helped them pick out toys that gave them their first orgasm. I've given sexuality workshops, written advice columns, and produced educational videos meant to empower everyone to take charge of their own sexuality without shame.

Growing up in such a supportive environment left me capable and in a position to fight for the voices and rights of others who were not so lucky.

When that knowledge is suppressed and young people are given the campaign of shame instead, bad things happen. My mother almost had a heart attack when she got her first period, because she thought she was bleeding to death. No one, including her mother, had told her about it.

In households where sex is shameful and not talked about, I see children being sexually abused and the abuse swept under the table. All we have to do is look at the rampant sexual abuse of young boys in the Catholic church to see an extreme example of this. I find that I am in the lucky 5% of women I've met who have *not* been sexually molested as a child. And a large percentage of my male friends were abused as well! All were shamed into hiding it.

The less sexuality is part of our social dialogue, the more chances those in positions of lesser power (women and children especially) will have it used as a weapon against them.

Denying and hiding sexuality does more harm than good. Studies show that abstinence-based sex ed in schools is less effective in preventing teen pregnancy and STDs than no sex education at all. Because abstinence-based sex ed programs are completely based in fundamentalist and Catholic Christian morality, they actually teach you not to use condoms and birth control. They teach that condoms are unreliable and actively discourage their use.

These programs result in more STDs and more young lives ruined by unwanted pregnancy — exactly what they supposedly set out to prevent.

FEARING ONESELF

I don't think the censors are protecting the children as much as they are protecting themselves from the corrupting influence of the naked body. It gives them feelings they are ashamed of, feelings that remind them they have a body, that make them fearful some women might take control of them with their sexuality. Did you ever notice that the most vehement attackers on sexuality are the ones most often caught in some child porn or other sexual scandal?

And here's the really ridiculous part: we all know men (and some women) are vast consumers of porn. Let's not lie: if you're a man, you almost certainly like and use porn. I believe there is absolutely nothing wrong with this. Your sexual pleasure is your own to pursue without shame, as long as it is not hurting anyone else. My husband uses porn up to three times a day, and I never feel threatened. Erotica exists. We should stop denying it.

Naked boobies and other naked bits flood the Internet daily. It is unfortunate that the censors are so ashamed of their own porn use that breasts are automatically assumed to be both sexual and shameful.

We are bombarded constantly by sex in our media, because it is a powerful selling tool. Hypersexualization occurs at a young age because that's what's cool and hip. We live in a fucked up society that is saturated by sexual images, yet tells us that sex is bad and shameful. This potent cocktail of arousal and shame serves to keep us good little sheeple, hating our urges and ourselves and keeping us laden with guilt.

To which I say: let the nakedness begin! Let the dialogue about sexuality come out into the open! If my own breasts are such a feared weapon against the establishment, then I will indeed use them to light the fuse!

CHANGE YOUR CONSCIOUSNESS WITH MAGIC

I am an atheist and a scientist, as are many Satanists, yet I also practice magic. I don't find this to be a paradox, because to me, reality itself is the most magical thing in the universe. My magic practices serve to act on my own subconscious, to help me move through reality with all my psychological levels aligned to a common goal.

I have found that magic is highly unique and personal. It's like a set of keys unique only to my consciousness, and nobody else's. Most of us have our own path that includes different rituals and magic that work for us; here I just want to provide a glimpse into my own experience.

LIVING A SACRED LIFE

In 2011, I made a vow to live my life full-time as a priestess and magician. I vowed to live in sacred space every second of every day. I vowed not to some external force, but instead to the forces I want to embody in every moment: love, truth, justice, compassion, destruction and renewal, transformation. I have not wavered from this vow.

In this path, magic is an integral part of what I do. In fact, I try to make every act a magical one, full of intent. In addition to my day-to-day magic, I also perform rituals to mark the moon phases and sun cycles, to honor my menstrual cycle, to set intention for a project, and to open up the inner gates of destruction in the service of transformation and renewal.

SPEAKING TO YOUNGER SELF

I perform magic not to change the outside world, but to change my own consciousness. In many ways, magic is just another tool to improve your own well-being. It works in ways much like meditation, massage, yoga, sex, and drugs: it produces a change in your outlook, often in your body, and most certainly in your subconscious.

We are more than just the flicker of our conscious mind. There are layers and layers of subconscious, memory, embedded mental models, and more that guide our thoughts and actions. We also have somatic body systems — breathing, fight or flight response, heart rate, brainwave patterns, and so on, that make up our complete self.

Magic is a way to involve far more of the self than just the regular conscious mind. One of my teachers referred to the unconscious parts of the mind as the Younger Self: the more primitive and in many cases more powerful parts that lie below simple logic and reason. Younger Self responds to emotion, to color and song and dance, to symbols, to repetitive chants. My ritual work speaks directly to Younger Self, to the parts of my brain that are older than civilization.

ALIGNING ALL PARTS

I use magic to create a certain state of mind, to imbue every moment with a sense of import, and to align all my multiple levels of consciousness in one direction, in service to one united intent.

Think of a screwdriver. If you run a magnet over it repeatedly in the same direction, it will become magnetized, all its atoms lined up along magnetic lines. With this unified alignment, the screwdriver gains the added power of being able to pick up dropped screws.

I use magic to align all parts of myself in whatever direction I intend. Sometimes the intention is to create a stable scaffolding to my life, as in my daily practices of meditation, dedication to the forces I serve, and mindfulness in every act. Sometimes it is to succeed at something specific: success at work, successful completion of an art project, fixing my back pain. In these cases, the ritual helps me commit to doing the hard, unpleasant work required to reach my goal.

Other magic is focused on aligning me with the external world. I grew up in the woods, and I've always felt the forces of nature running strong in me. I feel the need to stitch myself back into nature and the natural world by observing the moon cycles and seasons, by calling up the elemental forces inside me, and getting in touch with my very primal unconscious side via sex and blood magic. This anchors me to what I consider "the real world," the natural world that lies outside human civilization.

Some rituals are a complete abandonment of intent, for maximum creative inspiration without preconception. I use pain and cutting to let all the chaotic dark things inside my subconscious come pouring out in ritual space, where they leave their mark on the art I create there.

In the Satanic Bible, Anton LaVey called ritual space "The Psychic Decompression Chamber." I see ritual as the place I can unbind all restrictions on all levels of my consciousness, the place I can ignite the fires that will burn up and down all parts of my soul, the method by which I can point my actions both knowingly and unknowingly towards the places I want to go.

RITUAL AS AN EFFECTIVE TOOL

Some people rise early and plan their day out over coffee in their morning ritual. Some have lucky rabbit feet or a special rhyme they say before a game. Ritual is a very effective tool for reaching your potential and overcoming the most intimidating challenges, no matter what form it takes. A recent article in Scientific American studied this phenomenon:

> "Recent research suggests that rituals may be more rational than they appear. Why? Because even simple rituals can be extremely effective. Rituals performed after experiencing losses – from loved ones to lotteries – do alleviate grief, and rituals performed before high-pressure tasks – like singing in public – do in fact reduce anxiety and increase people's confidence. What's more, rituals appear to benefit even people who claim not to believe that rituals work." [10]

THE ARTIST AS MAGICIAN

All art I do is a magical act, and not just the art done in a ritual setting. Every word I write is a magical act, flung out into the web of many consciousnesses like a dandelion seed in search of soil. Every poem is a spell. Every photograph is an homage to the magic inherent in one fleeting moment, a ghost of life still flickering with slow pale fire. All my creative paths are aligned with my intent: to bring more love and joy into the world, to knock down decrepit walls with the truth, to dance on the ruins of the old structures of oppression and hate.

I'm not alone here. I believe every one of you who creates anything is a powerful magician. Before a groundbreaking advance or cultural shift is realized, it must first be birthed in someone's mind as an idea. Creation at any level is a magical act.

Let me end with a quote by Alan Moore, the renowned writer for some of my favorite comics, including Watchmen and V for Vendetta:

> *"There is some confusion as to what magic actually is. I think this can be cleared up if you just look at the very earliest descriptions of magic. Magic in its earliest form is often referred to as 'the art.' I believe this is completely literal. I believe that magic is art and that art, whether it be writing, music, sculpture, or any other form is literally magic.*
>
> *Art is, like magic, the science of manipulating symbols, words, or images, to achieve changes in consciousness. ... Indeed, to cast a spell, is simply to spell, to manipulate words, to change people's consciousness. And I believe that this is why an artist or writer is the closest thing in the contemporary world that you are likely to see to a Shaman." [11]*

—Alan Moore

OPEN-SOURCE YOUR MAGIC

Magic is not a part of everyone's Satanic path. But for many of us, it provides a much needed method to reach our own subconscious power. In some sense, it's a technology, a tool for getting what we want.

The Satanic Bible was one of the first mass-market paperbacks to openly discuss the details of ritual and magic. Until the last century, the details of magic, ceremony and shamanism were driven deep underground and shrouded in impenetrable mystery, unavailable to most seekers. Magical traditions and practices by necessity became secret with the rise of Christianity and other intolerant religions.

Practicing whatever magic you knew generally resulted in a slow and tortured death; even the hint that you might know something was usually a death warrant. No wonder ceremonial magic and hermetic mysteries were passed down in secrecy, while native shamanic and feminine traditions completely disappeared from any record.

But today, it's a little different. I'm not saying you can openly flaunt your Satanic beliefs and / or magical traditions in any circumstances without negative consequences. But the rise of social media and the free flow of information has created an incredible opportunity for us to share our beliefs and practices openly with each other, and even — dare I say it — the public. Let the exchange of ideas and heretofore secret, personal magical approaches begin!

I call this approach "Open Source Magic," and it's been a powerful method for me.

WHAT IS OPEN SOURCE?

The term "open source" comes from the software development community, and describes a collaborative method of creation:

> "In production and development, open source is a philosophy, or pragmatic methodology that promotes free redistribution and access to an end product's design and implementation details." [12]

Much of the Web is built on open source-based software like Linux. Mozilla Firefox is open source, as is the Android operating system. Many other Google technologies are based on open source foundations.

Open source software differs greatly from "proprietary" software (think Microsoft and Apple products), where code is hidden and copyrighted for maximum profits to the parent company:

> "Generally, open source refers to a program in which the source code is available to the general public for use and/or modification from its original design. Open source code is typically created as a collaborative effort in which programmers improve upon the code and share the changes within the community. Open source sprouted in the technological community as a response to proprietary software owned by corporations." [13]

WHY OPEN SOURCE MAGIC?

I choose my spiritual path and magical practices based solely on pragmatism: do they work for me? And by work, I don't mean making spooky things

happen out there in the world; I mean work by ful-
filling me, motivating me, changing my perspective,
aligning my consciousness and subconscious, or
otherwise serving me directly in some manner.

I have often heard "chaos magic" described this
way: you use what works for you, no matter what
the source. LaVey recognized this, though he did
also promote a certain framework for specifically
Satanic rituals:

> *"Satanic ritual is highly variable, with a basic
> format given in The Satanic Bible. Satanists are
> encouraged to use whatever props and means
> suit their immediate emotional and psychological
> needs in order to bring their workings to an
> exhausting and complete climax."* [14]

Practically, the more ideas I have access to, the
more powerful my rituals become, because I have
far more options to draw on. And while you can
conduct exhaustive historical research into traditions and archetypes using a service like Wikipedia,
I think sharing our own personal experiences with
magic is even more powerful.

The personal is *most* powerful, in my view. If
some of us decide to put our personal approaches
out there for the rest of us to see, I believe we'll con-
tribute to the greater reservoir of power available to
all. This is what I call "open-sourcing" magic.

But there's a second major practical reason for
me: instead of draining power away from my rituals
(as proponents of secret esoteric traditions often
claim), making them public gives them more power.
I am a creature of technology and the social web,

and I use its strands to draw attention, to give the LaVeyan command "Look." When the photos, video and documentation of my ritual reach an observing eye, they echo in that mind an image of the ritual, adding to its power across space and time.

My open sharing is also my act of service. If sharing my own experience and ideas can help anyone in any way, I am pleased.

A MAGICAL BLOG

I'm a firm follower of R. Buckminster Fuller's advice: "To change something, build a new model that makes the existing model obsolete." I choose to break the walls that hide my spiritual and magical path from the public, and make it openly accessible via a public blog. I am passionate about transparency and the free exchange of ideas, magic and art, and I want to lead by example.

My blog covers all aspects of my life, because I have vowed to live 100% in sacred space; thus everything I do is in service to my spiritual path. I put my magic, art and life out there publicly for all to see, without shame or fear. It is truly open source. I don't care if you use it for ideas, share it, or ignore it. My goal is to put it out there on the off-chance it might be helpful to someone else.

The scientific community has made a similar move they call Open Access; universities like MIT are starting to put more and more of their courses online, completely free. They've moved towards Open Access for the same reasons I have: because we treasure knowledge and want to share it, spread it, and let the collision and evolution of ideas occur across vast distances in the electronic space.

I keep my magical blog at SerpentsBlood.Tumblr. com. I encourage you to open-source your own path! Share your own experiences and magical ideas. The more of us that do it, the stronger we will be.

SOCIAL MEDIA MAGIC I

*"Learning to effectively utilize the
command to LOOK, is an integral part of
a witch's or warlock's training." [15]*

The rise of social media has given us an unprec-
edented opportunity to tap into the extremely powerful forces of our own personal charisma. We now
have 24/7, all-points access to a constant audience.
It only makes sense to apply magical, conscious
intent to how we use this new tool in the service of
our own personal Will.

LaVey calls to our attention the power our own
image has in all our interactions with others. There
is great power that one can wield for change in one's
life by making each interaction with another person
a conscious magical act.

A NETWORKED WEB OF ATTENTION

Think about your interaction with other people
in your daily life. How many of them actually care
about what you say, who you are, what you are really like? Your interaction with most people in the
physical world will be purely at the superficial level,
where they might notice how you look, but otherwise you don't even register as another person in
their limited monkey-verse.

Now compare your online interactions. The
nature of social media allows us to instantly connect
and share along multiple and unlimited avenues:
interests, beliefs, humor, music tastes, gender, social
justice causes, education, and existing personal
relationships.

This network of connections is extremely powerful, partly due to the "network effect," outlined by Bob Metcalfe. Metcalfe's law of technology states that the value of a telecommunications network is proportional to the square of the number of connected users of the system.

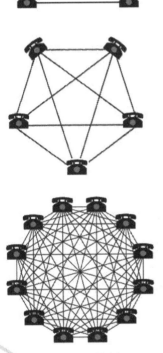

Metcalfe's Law states that the value of a telecommunications network is proportional to the square of the number of connected users of the system (n^2).

For instance, 2 telephones can make only 1 connection, 5 can make 10 connections, and 12 can make 66 connections.

Image courtesy of Wikipedia.

That is to say, the value and power of digital content, technologies and even magic grows exponentially with each single addition to the user base. The larger the network, the larger the power it has. It is the opposite of a scarcity-based economy, where more users equals fewer resources. Instead, the more users that are part of a network, the more valuable it becomes to each and every user.

In January 2014, Facebook, the largest social network, had 1.23 billion users worldwide. The potential to connect with other humans across the globe is astronomical, and exponentially growing.

REWARDS AWAIT

Every time someone encounters a piece of you online, there is an interaction and an opportunity for magic to do its work. Someone is actively interested in what you have to say, what you're about, maybe even who you are. Your audience is invested. They have obeyed the command to look.

It is up to you to consciously put in place the magic work to ensure that when the look occurs, what you will to be seen is seen. Because although it may only take place in the virtual world, the interactions that take place over social media can lead to huge real-world rewards: a new job, a date or a whole relationship, world-changing projects, gatherings of like-minded people in the real world. You may find immense social support and friendship as you become part of multiple self-organized communities that share your passions, your paths, your heartbreaks, your humor and more.

The world is your oyster when you have at

your fingertips the ability to instantly plug into the networked mind. Data was only the first thing to explode on the network. Now emotions, social interaction and real life-changing potential has found its way into the equation, and the network has come to life. Tap into its power!

SOCIAL MEDIA MAGIC II

Your first step in harnessing the magical power of social media will be to go inward and define who you are. To be effective, whatever you project must be true. In fact, you will encounter the greatest success by being truly yourself.

This is in accordance with the Satanic belief that we are all Gods, divine just as we are. In fact, our most natural self is the truest, most powerful being in our own universe, as long as we can unburden it from all the artificial guilt and fear imposed by society and religion.

CREATING A PERSONAL SELF MAP

Every time you make a posting to a social media network or interact with someone online, you are potentially making an impression. To carry mindfulness into these interactions, you need to become conscious of what you are projecting, and what you would like to project.

But before that, you need to figure out who you really are, what matters to you, what drives you and where your heart lies. I like to use a technique called "mind-mapping" for uninhibited brainstorming sessions.

"A mind map is a diagram used to visually outline information. A mind map is often created around a single word or text, placed in the center, to which associated ideas, words and concepts are added. Major categories radiate from a central node, and lesser categories are sub-branches of larger branches. Categories can represent words, ideas, tasks, or other items related to a central key word or idea." [16]

Here is the ritual that I used for my own magical mind map of my true self. I expect yours will be completely different in accordance with whatever magic works for you.

MIND MAP RITUAL

I set a sacred space boundary by donning my Baphomet pendant and drawing a circle with my ritual knife. I started by marking the paper with my blood, then wrote my name as the center with my ritual pen. I painted ink in a spiral out from my name.

I also had my priest Uruk sign his name and mark the paper with his blood, because we work together on all things in life. I circled both our names in my blood to denote this close relationship.

Then I began the mind mapping, extending out from my name in branches demarcating interests, important parts of my life, jobs, my artistic avenues, and my goals. This helped me see the structure of my life as I would like it to be. It laid it out in a non-hierarchical visual way, to help me understand my priorities, strengths, and options.

I ended by having both myself and my husband sign it with our personal demonic sigils.

CREATING YOUR PERSONALITY TRAIT LIST

Now that I had a clearer picture of what I wanted to work on via my relationships, both online and

in person, I could focus on the personality traits I would most like to support in myself. I made a list of traits I admire in others and the traits I would like to encourage in myself.

MAGICAL INTENT

I put these two documents over my laptop to help me be mindful in all my interactions, and to inspire me. I refer to them and keep them in mind in my day-to-day social media posts and interactions.

Note that this process is not directed at controlling other people's reactions to you. Nor is it about creating a false image. I intentionally live an incredibly integrated, open-to-public-viewing life. It's part of my magical path: the viewer is invited to participate in my magic simply by viewing.

You probably will want to choose more carefully which parts you want to show to the world, or to a network of friends. Determine if you need to emphasize different parts of you in different forums. For instance, people often let loose with their friends on Facebook but keep their LinkedIn work-related profiles strictly professional.

Apply the principles of conscious intent to your online interactions, keep all of them real and true to your self, and your social media experience will align with your true will.

THE SUSTENANCE OF DICHOTOMIES

Sometimes when I am in need of inspiration or a new perspective, I open the Satanic Bible to a random page and read it. This happened one night when I was struggling mightily with my innate dichotomy between wild and crazy abandon and scientific reason-mind. This is the reading I happened to turn to:

> "The Sixteenth Enochian Key gives recognition of the wondrous contrasts of the earth, and of the sustenance of these dichotomies." [17]

THE SIXTEENTH KEY: CREATION FROM DICHOTOMIES

Immediately my problem was framed as a solution. I recognized in the number sixteen the sixteen personality types, engendered by four core dichotomies, that make up the Myers-Briggs personality set. In non-psychiatry speak: I recognized that the great range of diversity often arises from a set of dichotomies. Think of our genetic code, giving rise to endless variation from two sets of genes.

My internal dichotomies were the source of my creativity, not my enemy. I could recognize my extremely opposite poles as a creative strength, not an obstacle.

A LEGACY OF CARL JUNG

I first encountered the Myers-Briggs test while working for a web startup in 1996. I took the test and the results seemed impressively accurate to me, even down to the careers suggested for me (journalism and activism). When I encountered the Satanic reading, I realized this test has magical significance for me.

The Myers-Briggs test is based on the theories of Carl Jung. Central to Jung's theories was the idea of individuation –

> *"the psychological process of integrating the opposites, including the conscious with the unconscious, while still maintaining their relative autonomy. Jung considered individuation to be the central process of human development."* [18]

Jung has relevance to the Satanic path because he saw clearly that those who could not face their shadow and integrate it fully would suffer repeatedly when they projected their unfaced fears and darkness onto the world. He saw integration of all one's dichotomies, including the shadow side, as essential to spiritual maturation.

In his 1921 book "Psychological Types," Jung expanded on his individuation theory by identifying different psychological types who used different modalities to cope with the world. In the 1940s, Katharine Cook Briggs and her daughter Isabel Briggs Myers formulated a psychology test based on Jung's theories of types. The test was originally created during World War II to help women who were entering the industrial workforce for the first time identify which war-time job would be most comfortable and effective for them.

RECOGNIZING THE DIVERSITY OF WORLDVIEWS

The test was designed to measure psychological preferences in how people perceive the world and make decisions. It is based on the theory that people have different ways of dealing with the world.

> "Personality typing as defined by Myers and Briggs assumes that much of our personality can be defined by dividing it into four independent preference areas or scales: energizing, attending, deciding, and living. Within each scale we have a preference for one of two opposites that define the scale. This makes for a total of 16 different combinations, each of which defines one particular and unique personality archetype." [19]

I found the test to give me results that described me and my ways of dealing with the world fairly accurately; for instance, it pinpointed my love of writing and my extroversion.

But the most important take-away I received from the test was simply realizing that not everyone was like me inside. It was a revelation that people have different toolsets they use to move through life. If you take the test and do some basic reading about the different types and modes, you'll soon be struck by just how different people's toolsets can be.

That realization can be the basis for more effective interactions with other people in your life, bringing you friendship and bounty. Once you realize how different people's approaches can be, you no longer try to make sense of their actions based solely on your own approach, and this helps develop a better understanding and connection.

And out of this test experience, you can see how many very different types can be created from a simple set of four dichotomies. For it is this sustenance of dichotomies, the diversity that is creating itself all the time around us simply from the interplay of opposites, that lends beauty and motion to the world.

In my personal life, I will no longer fear the extreme opposites that threaten to tear me apart from the inside. I will recognize the creative depths roiled up by those storms instead, and use them as inspiration.

You can easily find short, free versions of the Myers-Briggs test online with a web search. My type is ENFP, "the Champion."

114

EMBRACING REALITY

I believe there are two steps required for maximum effectiveness in creating the life you want. The Satanic path encourages us to take both these steps.

The first step to full empowerment is to recognize that you are your own God, as outlined in the Satanic Bible. I believe it's one of Satanism's most important messages. Nobody but yourself will save you, change your life, and fulfill your desires. You have full power to make the changes you want in your own life. You also have the full responsibility for realizing your own happiness. No one else is going to do it for you.

You've accepted that you are fully empowered. Now what? Step two is not as obvious, but equally important: recognizing and accepting the reality around you.

To become fully effective in changing your world, you must have the most accurate picture of it possible. You must awaken completely to the present, the only place where you can exercise your power. You must open your awareness to all things as they are — not as you think they are, not as someone else tells you they are, and not as you think they should be!

Without an accurate picture of the canyon, the bridge builder cannot build a functioning bridge. So too is it with all our actions. We may charge ahead blindly, armed with our firmly held beliefs, but reality all too often will sideswipe us if we don't give it the respect it deserves. Seeing the world you move in accurately is the key to changing it or coping with it.

CUTTING AWAY THE BLINDERS

How do we begin sharpening our awareness of the world as it is? We can certainly take a page from the story of Satan himself. Satan's rebellion symbolizes the power to question, no matter how sacred the cow. Satanism cuts through the calcified structures of old belief systems that have held the human race in thrall for centuries. It dares to point out the hypocrisy and lies built by man in the name of God.

Take this questioning attitude to all arenas of your life, not just religion. Question all assumptions, all presumptions. Leave your own prejudices at the door. Enter each situation with an open mind, determined to observe things as they are instead of coming in with preconceptions.

I struggle with this in my own life. It's easy to think I have an accurate model of what's going on in my life. As a scientist and mathematician, I've learned that models can be extremely helpful. But in real life, not everything fits neatly into a predictive model. My human brain wants to see patterns where there are none. My fears whisper to me about future calamities and give me an inaccurate picture of my progress. I have learned that assumptions are always a bad idea.

I've learned that to see truth and reality, you must discard the screens that cloud your vision. Think of Kali with her sharp sword, ready to cut away the illusions that chain you to suffering. Turn that sword on your own set of assumptions.

Zen Buddhism speaks of the Child Mind, open and questioning, with no preconceptions. The Child Mind simply wants to learn. This is the state we strive to achieve in every moment, receptive to new information and experiences.

To reach this state, you must be willing to let go of ego attachments to what you think you know. Many people have a heavy ego investment in being right.

I can always tell when someone has a flexible mind without heavy ego attachment by using one simple test. If I use a big word in conversation and they ask me what it means, it shows me they value learning over "saving face." In other words, they aren't afraid to look stupid if it means they will learn something new. Be one of those people! Leave your ego behind and simply observe the world as it is. Ask questions, because otherwise you'll never learn new things.

LISTEN TO ALL YOUR VOICES

The reliance on our intellect alone can also get in the way of unobstructed observation. We are used to thinking of our forebrain, our center of conscious higher reasoning, as the ultimate authority on reality. But the forebrain can get wrapped up chasing its own tail. We tend to second-guess ourselves and our perceptions, or overthink them to death.

Don't just take your forebrain's word for it: listen to what the rest of you has to say too. Your lizard brain, where intuition and instinct are processed, is also a finely tuned instrument for coping with the world. Your unconscious contains far more information than your conscious mind can see. You've heard this as "trust your gut." If you can silence the irrelevant chatter of the conscious mind, you'll be able to better grasp the world as it flows in constant change around you.

ENGAGING WITH THE WORLD VIA FLOW

Other techniques will help you anchor yourself in reality as well. Though it seems counterintuitive, losing yourself completely in an activity means you have engaged completely in reality and are effortlessly moving in the flow of the present. Psychologists call this "flow":

> *"Flow is completely focused motivation. It is a single-minded immersion and represents perhaps the ultimate experience in harnessing the emotions in the service of performing and learning. In flow, the emotions are not just contained and channeled, but positive, energized, and aligned with the task at hand. To be caught in the ennui of depression or the agitation of anxiety is to be barred from flow. The hallmark of flow is a feeling of spontaneous joy, even rapture, while performing a task, although flow is also described as a deep focus on nothing but the activity – not even oneself or one's emotions."* [20]

I find flow in writing, but everyone has their personal passion that brings them into flow space. In flow, I let whatever is inside find its way out naturally to a place I can see it more clearly. Once I've put my thoughts and feelings into words on a page, I can look at them more objectively and better understand my own reality.

EXERCISE YOUR ATTENTION

Simple meditation can help free your mind from the ceaseless chatter that stands in the way of experiencing reality as it happens in real time. I practice mindfulness meditation every day for 20 minutes.

I credit this daily practice for much of my sanity, clarity, and performance levels.

Scientific studies support meditation's ability to increase your powers of observation, attention and reaction, while also reducing stress. One 2007 study showed that meditation increased attention by allowing your mind to let go of thoughts more quickly so you can process what is going on right in front of you:

> "'It appears that the ability to release thoughts that pop into mind frees the brain to attend to more rapidly changing things and events in the world at large,' said the study's lead author, Richard Davidson. Expert meditators, he said, are better than other people at detecting such fast-changing stimuli, like emotional facial expressions." [21]

Meditating can actually physically build up your brain in crucial areas, as shown in a 2010 study:

> "The researchers report that those who meditated for about 30 minutes a day for eight weeks had measurable changes in gray-matter density in parts of the brain associated with memory, sense of self, empathy and stress. M.R.I. brain scans taken before and after the participants' meditation regimen found increased gray matter in the hippocampus, an area important for learning and memory. The images also showed a reduction of gray matter in the amygdala, a region connected to anxiety and stress." [22]

Fortunately, mindfulness meditation is extremely easy and doesn't require any special trappings, incense, chants or gurus. Here's how I practice it:

Sit comfortably but upright in a chair, on the floor, or wherever you prefer. Place your hands in your lap facing up. You can choose to leave your eyes open, but not focused on any one thing. I usually close my eyes. Set a timer — anywhere from 3 minutes to an hour. I find 15 minutes is enough to make a big difference in my daily life. Make sure you won't be interrupted by anything else.

Begin by bringing your awareness to yourself and setting a simple intention. I use "I am now doing something to support my own well-being." Then gently bring your attention to your breath. Don't try to change it; just observe as it rises and falls. Your goal is to keep your attention on your breath throughout the meditation. I find it helpful to imagine that I'm resting my attention on the breath as one would rest on a mattress or a tree branch, feeling it rise and fall under me.

Thoughts will certainly arise and begin to flood up into your brain. Acknowledge them as they form, but let them go without attachment or judgement and return your attention back to your breathing with kindness and gentleness.

Any time your mind strays, return it with this kindness. Each time you do this, you are strengthening your "attention muscle," just as you would strengthen an arm muscle in the gym. I've found that simply sitting with yourself in loving kindness like this does a great deal of healing all on its own.

After you practice this for a while, you'll notice your brain disengages from the racing thoughts more easily, leaving you in a state of flow as the present moves through your awareness.

When the timer goes off, take a few breaths to return to the regular world. That's it! It will actually be hard at first, but stick with it. Eventually a daily meditation practice can equip you with a better mental toolset to experience reality as it flows by in every moment.

USE YOUR VOICE

"Non serviam! (I will not serve!)" With these words, say the legends, Satan spoke out against God in rebellion. Not content to quietly accept his forced servitude, he spoke up and voiced his true will, breaking forever with a Heaven built on lies and flattery.

Likewise, your voice is equally powerful. Use it as the powerful tool it is: a sharp blade of truth that cuts away obstacles in your path and topples the encrusted lies of a corrupt system.

THE SATANIC VOICE

The very foundations of Satanism emphasize speaking up in the face of falsehoods. In "The Satanic Bible," Anton LaVey writes: "No hoary falsehood shall be a truth to me; no stifling dogma shall encramp my pen! .... Whenever, therefore, a lie has built unto itself a throne, let it be assailed without pity and without regret, for under the domination of an inconvenient falsehood, no one can prosper."

Christianity teaches us to be good followers, to refrain from questioning, to just sit quietly and obey the priest. Mass culture also promotes a quiet acceptance of the system we've built ourselves into: work, suffer, consume, repeat. Our rebellion and need for self-expression has been co-opted by marketers and sold back to us; individuality now means wearing a certain brand of jeans. Good sheeple are taught to passively accept, buy, obey, and keep their mouth shut.

But Satanists are a different breed. We have seen

behind the veil to the lies, greed and hate at the core of the Abrahamic religions that dominate so many people. We are not afraid to speak the truth. We are not afraid to point out that the emperor has no clothes.

And when we do, the others around us may realize just how far the lies go and wake up from their sheepledom.

THE POWER OF TRUTH IN ACTION

I saw a direct example of this last summer, when my husband Uruk and I visited Hempfest, a cannabis festival in Seattle. As we walked in the gates, we passed a group of hatemongering protestors from a fundamentalist church. They were shouting angrily at festival-goers, urging us all to repent from our drug-loving ways, trying to force their God on us with shame, guilt and hate.

My husband did not keep quiet and try to ignore the hate directed at us, as I did. Instead he said, "I don't care what your God thinks; I'm a Satanist." They immediately engaged with him, trying to persuade him to stop worshipping Satan. His response? "Satanists don't worship Satan."

They tried to argue back with him that yes, he did. So he asked if any of them had actually read the Satanic Bible. Of course they said no. He replied, "Then you don't have any right to say anything about my religion. If you want me to respect yours, respect mine. Read the literature first, and then I'd be happy to have a rational discussion." We walked away without a second thought and enjoyed ourselves at the festival.

As we left, however, the team of Hempfest volunteers came running up to us, breathless with thanks. Apparently, the hate-filled church protestors had been so embarrassed by Uruk's calm, reasonable response that they left in a flustered huff, saving the poor festival-goers and staff from further vitriol. My husband spoke up in the face of lies and hate, and it made a real difference.

THE TRUTH IS IN YOUR HANDS

I believe our political and financial systems are corrupt down to the very root, filled with lies built on lies built on lies. And the masses who give them their power are woefully ignorant of this web of lies, because our system lacks transparency and the accountability that might be demanded were the truth to suddenly come to light. Transparency and accountability are the two most important guides to any organization that hopes to remain flexible and functioning for the good of all members. The organizations that run our current world are lacking both.

And we can't turn to our traditional truthbringers for help. The media long ago went under the control of large corporate interests, which are tied to the political and banking machines. Real journalism is virtually dead; it just doesn't pay. The public wants cute pictures of cats and Hollywood celebrity news. CNN fired most of its journalists and is instead using user-submitted "news." Fox News won the right to lie outright in a 2010 court case. Don't turn to the media to bring you the truth.

This is why it's so vital for you to use your voice. Nothing will change until someone speaks up — and that someone is you.

SPEAK UP FOR YOURSELF

Learn to speak up for yourself and your own needs. This is a fundamental tenet of Satanism, that you must take care of yourself first. And your voice is one of your most potent tools in getting all that you desire. Learn to communicate directly and clearly, without taking things personally or trying to control other people. An honest communicator is far more successful in all arenas: work, love, sex, home life.

I had to learn this the hard way. I am a conflict avoider. I used to go to ridiculous lengths to avoid conflict with another person. But I'm slowly learning to face conflict when it is required in the service of the truth or to get my needs met.

I was taught when I was very young to put other people's needs above my own, because humility was the greatest service to God. Even when I shed the lies of Christianity, this people-pleasing nature was still firmly ingrained in me. Coupled with my aversion to conflict, it meant I would let something sit silently and fester inside for hours, days, even years without saying anything about it.

Around 2000, I was working for Amazon.com, leading a team that was launching a new product line. I had been working there for two years and had been promoted several times, but my salary remained flat. I had meekly accepted this, thinking that was just the way things were, until at one review time I chose the raises for my team and found myself again wondering why I was being paid less than some of them.

I finally got up the guts to talk to my boss about

this and ask for a raise. His response? "Oh wow, I didn't even realize it was so low! Why didn't you say so sooner?" And immediately I was bumped up from $50k to $65k.

The old adage is true: if you don't ask, you'll never receive. Raise your voice about how you feel and what you need, and you may be pleasantly surprised at the results.

USE IT OR LOSE IT

If you don't speak up and use your voice, your right to use it will continue to be eroded away by a system that wants you to shut up and be a good little sheeple. It is no coincidence that the first thing a fascist government does is to take over the press. How could China maintain such a corrupt regime in this modern, connected world without basically stamping out open Internet access and substituting its own version? The US government is also rabid in its attempts to silence whistle-blowing journalists and curtail access to online information in the name of protecting big corporate interests.

Philosopher Edmund Burke wrote, "All that is necessary for the triumph of evil is that good men do nothing." If no one points out the emperor has no clothes, the lie will continue to harm. Take the courage and passion of your heart and put it into words. Use your voice. It is one of your most powerful tools.

Resources

SMART Recovery

A supportive group can be helpful in the right circumstances. If you are interested in a science-based recovery program that emphasizes self-empowerment, I recommend checking out Smart Recovery:

smartrecovery.org.

SMART Recovery's four-point program:
1. *Motivation to Abstain: Enhancing and maintaining motivation to abstain from addictive behavior*
2. *Coping with Urges: Learning how to cope with urges and cravings*
3. *Problem Solving: Using rational ways to manage thoughts, feelings and behaviors*
4. *Lifestyle Balance: Balancing short-term and long-term pleasures and satisfactions in life*

Opiate Addiction

If you or someone you know suffers from opiate addiction, buprenorphine (Suboxone) can help end it for good without the hell of withdrawal. You can find a listing of all doctors licensed to prescribe buprenorphine in the US, listed by state, at this website:

buprenorphine.samhsa.gov/bwns_locator/

Bibliography

[1] *The Satanic Temple;*
thesatanictemple.com 1

[2] Peter Gilmore, **churchofsatan.com.** 2

[3] *Satanic Ritual Abuse;* Wikipedia 18

[4] *What Is Cognitive Dissonance;*
about.com 34

[5] *How it Works;* Narcotics Anonymous. 42

[6] *Obama Administration releases
Third National Climate Assessment
for the US;* NOAA News 59

[7] *Just World Hypothesis;* Wikipedia 64

[8] *Just World Hypothesis;* Wikipedia 64

[9] *Men and Women's Differences Aren't
Actually Distinct, Confirms Study;*
Emma Gray, Huffington Post 71

[10] *Why Rituals Work;* Scientific American 88

[11] Alan Moore 89

[12] *Open Source;* Wikipedia 92

[13] *Open Source;* Wikipedia 92

[14] *LaVeyan Satanism;* Wikipedia 93

[15] *The Satanic Bible;* Anton LaVey 97

[16] *Mind Mapping;* Wikipedia 104

[17] *The Satanic Bible;* Anton LaVey 109

[18] *Carl Jung;* Wikipedia .110

[19] *Myers-Briggs Type Indicator;* Wikipedia 111

[20] *Flow;* Wikipedia. 118

[21] *Study Suggests Meditation Can Train
Attention;* Sandra Blakely,
New York Times, 2007 .119

[22] *How Meditation May Change the
Brain;* Sindya Bhanoo,
New York Times, 2011 .119

ILLUSTRATIONS

ABOUT THE AUTHOR

   Lilith Starr is a writer, photographer, blood artist and activist. She is the founding head of the Seattle chapter of the Satanic Temple. She holds a bachelor's degree in English Literature and Language from Harvard University and a master's degree in Journalism from Stanford University. She lives in Seattle with her husband and full-time slave, Uruk Black.

Book design donated by **lenakartzov.com**

End